POCKET **ROUGH GUIDE**
FLORENCE

written and researched by
JONATHAN BUCK

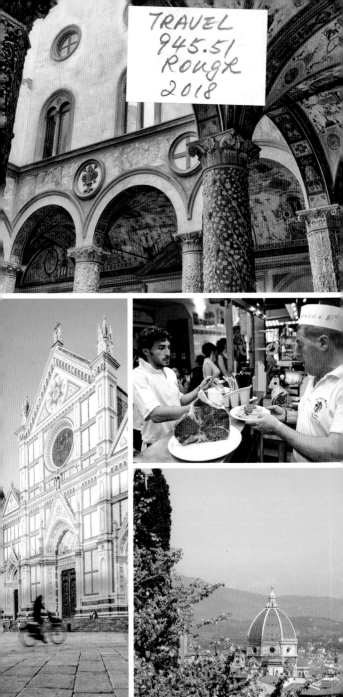

CONTENTS

Introduction 4

When to visit.. 6
Where to... 7
Florence at a glance 8
Things not to miss.. 10
Itineraries.. 18

Places 24

Piazza del Duomo and around................................. 26
Piazza della Signoria and around............................ 36
West of the centre 54
North of the centre.. 70
East of the centre 88
Oltrarno... 100
The city outskirts 120
Fiesole... 124

Accommodation 128

Hotels and residenze.. 130
Hostels.. 136
Camping... 137

Essentials 138

Arrival 140
Getting around... 140
Directory A–Z... 141
Festivals and events 145
Chronology.. 146
Italian... 149
Small print and index... 156

Clockwise from top: The Palazzo Vecchio; Trattoria Mario; the view from Villa Bardini; the Basilica di Santa Croce. Previous page: The Palazzo Vecchio and the Florence skyline

FLORENCE

If one city could be said to encapsulate the essence of Italy it might well be Florence (Firenze in Italian), the first capital of the united country. The modern Italian language evolved from Tuscan dialect, and Dante's Divina Commedia was the first great work of Italian literature to be written in the vernacular; but what makes this city pivotal to the culture not just of Italy but of all Europe is, of course, the Renaissance. The very name by which we refer to this extraordinary era was coined by a Tuscan, Giorgio Vasari, who wrote in the sixteenth century of the "rebirth" of the arts with the humanism of Giotto and his successors. Every eminent artistic figure from Giotto onwards – Masaccio, Donatello, Botticelli, Leonardo da Vinci, Michelangelo – is represented here, in an unrivalled concentration of churches, galleries and museums.

Ponte Vecchio at dusk

Mercato Centrale

What's new

For tourists, the most significant changes in Florence in recent years have been the opening of a whole new floor of the Uffizi galleries and the spectacular rebuilding of the Museo dell'Opera del Duomo. The city's main market, the Mercato Centrale, has also been transformed – it now houses a host of late-opening places to eat and drink. Bedevilled by controversy, the city's major infrastructure project – the tram network – proceeds slowly.

During the fifteenth century, architects such as Brunelleschi and Alberti began to transform the cityscape of Florence, raising buildings that were to provide future generations with examples from which to take a lead. As soon as you step out of the train station the imprint of the Renaissance is visible, with the pinnacle of Brunelleschi's stupendous dome visible over the rooftops, and the Renaissance emphasis on harmony is exemplified with unrivalled eloquence in Brunelleschi's interiors of **San Lorenzo**, **Santo Spirito** and the **Cappella dei Pazzi**, and in Alberti's work at Santa Maria Novella and the Palazzo Rucellai. In painting, the development of the new sensibility can be plotted stage by stage in the vast picture collection of the recently expanded **Uffizi**, while the **Bargello**, the **Museo dell'Opera del Duomo** and the mighty guild church of **Orsanmichele** do the same for the story of sculpture. Equally

revelatory are the fabulously decorated chapels of **Santa Croce** and **Santa Maria Novella**, forerunners of such astonishing creations as Masaccio's frescoes at **Santa Maria del Carmine**, Fra' Angelico's serene paintings at **San Marco**, and Andrea del Sarto's work at **Santissima Annunziata**, to name just a few. Florence is the city of Michelangelo, one of the dominant creative figures of sixteenth-century Italy, the scope of whose genius can only be appreciated after you've seen his astonishing San Lorenzo's **Sagrestia Nuova** and the marble statuary of the **Accademia** – home of the *David*. Michelangelo's two great rivals, Raphael and Titian, along with dozens of other supreme painters, are on show in the enormous art gallery of the **Palazzo Pitti,** once the home of the city's most famous family, the Medici, whose former home – the beautiful **Palazzo Medici-Riccardi** – can also be visited.

The Last Supper by Domenico Ghirlandaio, Museo di San Marco

The achievements of the Renaissance were of course underpinned by the wealth that had been accumulated in earlier decades by the Medici and Florence's other plutocratic dynasties, and in every quarter of the centre you'll see churches and monuments that attest to the financial might of medieval Florence: the Duomo, the Baptistery, the Palazzo Vecchio, the huge churches of Santa Croce and Santa Maria Novella, and the exquisite Romanesque gem of San Miniato al Monte are among the most conspicuous demonstrations of Florence's prosperity. As for the centuries that followed the heyday of the Renaissance, it's often forgotten that Florence played a major role in the development of modern science – this was, after all, the home of **Galileo**, whose name has been bestowed on the city's fascinating science museum.

It has to be said that nowadays it can often seem that Florence has become too popular for its own good. The city has been a magnet for tourists since the nineteenth century, when Stendhal staggered around its streets in a stupor of aesthetic delight, and nowadays, in high season, parts of the city can be almost unbearable, with immense queues for the Uffizi and pedestrian traffic at a standstill on the Ponte Vecchio. But if you time your visit carefully, don't rush around trying to see everything and make a point of eating and drinking in our recommended restaurants, cafés and bars, you'll have a visit you'll never forget.

When to visit

Midsummer in Florence can be less than pleasant: the heat is often stifling, and the inundation of tourists makes the major attractions a purgatorial experience. For the most enjoyable visit, arrive shortly before **Easter** or in **October**: the weather should be fine, and the balance between Florentines and outsiders restored to its rightful level. Winter is often quite rainy, but the absence of crowds makes this a good option for the big sights. If you can only travel between Easter and September, reserve your accommodation well before you arrive, as it's not uncommon for every hotel in the centre to be fully booked. The worst month is **August**, when the majority of Italians take their holidays, with the result that many restaurants and bars are closed for the month.

Where to...

Shop

Florence is known as a producer of **luxury items**, notably gold jewellery, high-quality leather goods, top-grade stationery and marbled paper. The whole Ponte Vecchio is crammed with goldsmiths, but the city's premier shopping thoroughfare is **Via de' Tornabuoni**, where you'll find the showrooms of Italy's top fashion designers. Prada, Gucci, Armani, Dolce & Gabbana are all here, as are the country's main outlets for three of the top Florentine fashion houses – Pucci, Roberto Cavalli and Ferragamo. For cheap and cheerful stuff there's the plethora of stalls around San Lorenzo, and there's also a handful of good **department stores**.

OUR FAVOURITES: Aqua Flor p.95. Barberino Designer Outlet p.123. Giulio Giannini e Figlio p.113.

Eat

As you'd expect in a major tourist city, Florence has plenty of restaurants, but – unsurprisingly – a large number of them are aimed squarely at outsiders, so standards are often patchy, especially around Piazza della Signoria and Piazza del Duomo. But several good-quality and good-value restaurants lie on the periphery of the city centre, notably around **Santa Croce** and **Sant'Ambrogio**, and across the river in **Oltrarno**. Simple meals are served in many Florentine bars and cafés, so if you fancy a quick bite to eat rather than a full-blown meal, take a look at our list of cafés and bars in each Places chapter of this guide.

OUR FAVOURITES: Ora d'Aria p.53. Io – Osteria Personale p.118. Il Guscio p.117.

Drink

As elsewhere in Italy, the distinction between Florentine bars and cafés can be tricky to the point of impossibility, as almost every café serves alcohol and almost every bar serves coffee. That said, some cafés have an emphasis on coffee and cakes, just as there are plenty of bars dedicated to the **wines** of the Tuscan vineyards. The humblest wine bars belong to the endangered species known as the **vinaio**, which consists of little more than a few shelves of workaday wines plus a counter of snacks. At the opposite pole there's the **enoteca**, which has a vast wine menu and often a good kitchen too.

OUR FAVOURITES: Fuori Porta p.114. Rex Caffè p.96. Volume p.116.

Go out

Many of Florence's hotter bars try to keep the punters on the premises by serving free snacks with the **aperitivi** (usually about 7–9pm) before the music kicks in – either live or (more often) supplied by a DJ. Florence is quite a sedate city, but like every university town it has some decent clubs and music venues. For up-to-the-minute **information** about what's on, pick up a copy of the *Firenze Spettacolo* monthly listings magazine or call in at Box Office, near the Sant'Ambrogio market at Via Delle Vecchie Carcere 1 (Mon–Fri 9.30am–7pm, Sat 9.30am–2pm; ⓦ boxofficetoscana.it) – it sells tickets for most events.

OUR FAVOURITES: Tenax p.123. YAB p.69. Blob Club p.53.

Fortezza da Basso

VIALE SPART

West of the centre p.54.

On the west side of the central zone you'll find Florence's big-money shopping street, Via de'Tornabuoni. Beyond here, the big draw is Santa Maria Novella, but there's plenty more to see, notably Ognissanti, Santa Trinita and the Musei Marino Marini.

Stazione Santa Maria Novella

Mercato Centrale

Santa Maria Novella

San Loren

Ognissanti

Museo Novecento

Museo Marino Marini

Baptistery

VIA DE'TORNABUON

PIAZZA DELLA REPUBBLICA

Palazzo Strozzi

Piazza del Duomo and around p.26.

Florence is a twin-nucleus city: one part for the church, one part for the city authorities. Piazza del Duomo, with the stupendous cathedral, baptistery and belltower, plus the superb Museo dell'Opera del Duomo, is the church's domain.

Santa Trinita

River Arno

PIAZZA DEL CARMINE
Santa Maria del Carmine

Santo Spirito

Santa Felicita

OLTRARNO

Oltrarno p.100.

Oltrarno, squeezed between the hills and the south bank of the river, has the city's biggest concentration of good bars and restaurants, especially around Piazza Santo Spirito and Piazza del Carmine. Culturally, it's a rich area too: in addition to Palazzo Pitti, you shouldn't miss the churches of Santo Spirito and San Miniato, nor the frescoes of the Cappella Brancacci, one of Italy's greatest treasures.

Palazzo Pitti

Forte di Belvedere

Florence at a glance

North of the centre p.70.
The Mercato Centrale is the commercial hub of the northern part of central Florence – and there are a lot of good places to eat and drink in the market area. For tourists, the Palazzo Medici-Riccardi, San Lorenzo and San Marco are the top three attractions. And Piazza Santissima Annunziata is one of the city's finest squares.

San Marco

Accademia

PIAZZA SANTISSIMA ANNUNZIATA

Museo Archeologico

Palazzo Medici-Riccardi

PIAZZA EL DUOMO

Duomo

Santa Maria Maddalena dei Pazzi

Teatro della Pergola

Piazza della Signoria and around p.36.
Dominated by the fortress-like Palazzo Vecchio, the handsome and spacious Piazza della Signoria is the political hub of Florence. The Uffizi gallery, right next door to the Palazzo Vecchio, makes this the number one spot on the tourist trail too.

Teatro Verdi

ZZA DELLA SIGNORIA

Palazzo Vecchio

Uffizi

PIAZZA SANTA CROCE

VIA DEI BENCI

Santa Croce

East of the centre p.88.
To the east the centre of gravity is the spacious Piazza Santa Croce, with its mighty church. In the evening, the bars and restaurants of this quarter make it one of the liveliest parts of town. For the under-30s, the bars of Via dei Benci are always a big draw. You'll also find some of the city's best gelati and pizzas here, alongside the priciest haute cuisine in the city.

17

Things not to miss

It's not possible to see everything that Florence has to offer in one trip – and we don't suggest you try. What follows is a selective taste of the city's highlights, from cultural and historic to the best places to eat and drink.

< The Duomo
p.26 & 30
Brunelleschi's magnificent dome, crowning the Duomo, is the city's defining image; the ancient Baptistery, alongside, is stunning, both inside and out.

< The Bargello
p.46
This stupendous museum of sculpture and applied arts is an essential complement to the Uffizi.

∨ San Marco
p.80
An extraordinary sequence of frescoes by Fra' Angelico adorns the cells and chapels of the San Marco monastery.

< The Palazzo Medici-Riccardi
p.76
Benozzo Gozzoli's delightful frescoes are the highlight of the huge Palazzo Medici-Riccardi.

> Wine bars
p.86 & p.115
With the Chianti vineyards on the doorstep, Florence is a great place to sample top-notch Italian vintages – be sure to visit wines bars such as Casa del Vino (p.86) and Le Volpi L'Uva (p.115).

> The Cappella Brancacci
p.109
The startling images created by Masaccio make the Brancacci chapel one of the most significant artistic monuments in Europe.

< **Santa Maria Novella**
p.62
Alberti's innovative facade fronts this art-packed church, featuring stunning frescoes by Uccello, Ghirlandaio, Masaccio and others.

∨ **The Museo dell'Opera del Duomo**
p.32
Ghiberti's "Gates of Paradise" plus masterpieces by Donatello and Michelangelo are on show in the new-look Museo dell'Opera del Duomo.

< **San Lorenzo**
p.70
The parish church of
the Medici has some
extraordinary Donatello
sculptures.

> **Santa Croce**
p.88
Glorious frescoes by Giotto
and the serene Pazzi
chapel are but two of the
treasures of the mighty
Santa Croce.

< **Uffizi**
p.42
The Uffizi is the finest gathering of Italian Renaissance art on the planet.

∨ **Santa Trìnita**
p.58
Some of the Medici have walk-on roles in Ghirlandaio's scenes from the life of St Francis, in Santa Trìnita.

< **The Palazzo Vecchio**
p.40
Take one of the "Secret Tours" to get the most out of the building from which Florence was governed.

> **Mercato Centrale**
p.77
A cornucopia of local produce, with plenty of places to eat and drink upstairs.

> **The Accademia**
p.78
Well, you can't come to Florence and not see the *David*, can you? Be sure to book your ticket in advance – there's always a queue.

< **San Miniato al Monte**
p.112
Overlooking the city from the south, the San Miniato is a masterpiece of Romanesque architecture.

∨ **Palazzo Pitti**
p.102
The Palatina art collection is second only to the Uffizi, and it's just one of the museums to be found in the colossal Pitti palace; and the palace's garden – the Bóboli – is gorgeous too.

Day One in Florence

The Uffizi p.42. The Uffizi is the obvious first stop: a mind-blowing parade of masterpieces, and it now has a whole new floor of galleries. If you're going in high season, make sure you book your ticket in advance or you face interminable queues.

Santa Croce p.88. The vast church of Santa Croce has amazing frescoes by Giotto and other masters, and the Pazzi Chapel is one of the finest pieces of Renaissance architecture in Italy.

🍽 Lunch in Sant'Ambrogio
Grab a bargain lunch in the market (p.95) – perhaps some salami, cheeses and biscotti – or drop in on Florence's best pizzeria, *Il Pizzaiuolo* (p.97).

Ponte Vecchio p.101. Take the picturesque route over the river into the Oltrarno district.

Palazzo Pitti p.102. You could spend all day in the Pitti, which has several museums under its roofs – the Palatina galleries are the absolute highlight, with wonderful paintings by Raphael, Titian and many others. The palace's garden is wonderful too.

Cappella Brancacci p.109. Masaccio's frescoes are epoch-defining creations.

🍷 Aperitivo
at *Slowly* (p.68), then a spot of dinner at *Oliviero* (p.69), followed by a nightcap at *Zoe* (p.116) or *Il Rifrullo* (p.115).

ITINERARIES

Santa Croce

Ponte Vecchio

Slowly

Day Two in Florence

The Bargello p.46. Get a crash-course in Renaissance sculpture: Michelangelo, Cellini, Donatello, Verrocchio – they are all here.

The Duomo p.26. The dome of the Duomo is one of the most amazing structures in all of Italy.

The Museo dell'Opera del Duomo p.32. Michelangelo's harrowing *Pietà*, a roomful of wonderful Donatellos, the *Doors of Paradise*, and much more.

Lunch *Yellow Bar* (p.53). It may not look enticing, but *Yellow Bar* is one of the best places in the city for an unpretentious meal.

San Lorenzo and Medici tombs p.70. There's yet more from Michelangelo and Donatello at the mausoleum of Florence's quasi-royal family – and don't miss the amazing library next door.

Santa Maria Novella and its museum p.62. Alberti's facade makes Santa Maria Novella perhaps the city's most handsome church, and a cornucopia of memorable art is to be found inside, including an exquisite fresco cycle by Ghirlandaio.

Aperitivo Cross the water for a drink *Dolce Vita* (p.114) then stroll over to the chic and innovative *Io – Osteria Personale* (p.118), one of the most interesting restaurants to have opened in the city for years.

The Duomo

Santa Maria Novella

Yellow Bar

Quiet Florence

Florence is one of Europe's busiest tourist destinations, but it's possible to escape the crowds, even in the centre of town. These places are rarely busy, and in the low season you could have some of them to yourself.

Museo Galileo p.44. Everybody knows about the art, but few visitors bother themselves with Florence's scientific heritage – this fascinating museum fills in the story.

Santi Apostoli p.55. This beautiful and ancient church is the most tranquil building in central Florence.

Santa Trìnita p.58. One of the chapels here has a gorgeous cycle of frescoes by Ghirlandaio.

Ognissanti p.66. It has a Giotto painting, a Botticelli and two works by Ghirlandaio, but Ognissanti is overlooked by the tour groups.

Lunch Buy your supplies at an *alimentari*, and wander out to the Cascine park (p.120) for a picnic lunch.

Santo Spirito p.108. Don't be deterred by the blank exterior – Brunelleschi's spacious and serene church is a marvel of Renaissance design.

Santa Felìcita p.101. Located just yards from the Ponte Vecchio, Santa Felìcita demands a visit for Pontormo's extraordinary *Deposition*.

San Miniato al Monte p.112. Climb the hill to visit this glorious Romanesque church, perhaps the most serene building in the city.

Evening in Oltrarno p.114 When it comes to eating and drinking, you're spoilt for choice on Florence's south bank but if it's a tranquil evening you're after, avoid Piazza Santo Spirito.

Museo Gallileo

Santi Apostoli

San Miniato al Monte

Shopping Florence

The home town of Gucci, Pucci and Ferragamo has plenty of outlets that cater for gold-card holders, as you'd expect, but there are also some places to tempt those on less exalted budgets.

Coin and Rinascente p.51 & p.35. Explore the city's two major department stores, finishing with a coffee on the roof of Rinascente.

San Lorenzo market p.86. The avenues of market stalls at San Lorenzo will keep you browsing for a while – and the food hall is irresistible.

🍴 **Lunch** *Da Mario* (p.87), located just yards from the market hall, is a real Florentine institution.

Farmacia di Santa Maria Novella p.67. Florence's most gorgeous (and aromatic) shop is worth a visit just to inhale the air. But buy a bar of soap, at least.

Via de' Tornabuoni p.59. Even if you can't afford a Pucci frock, window-shopping is fun on the city's designer row.

Giulio Giannini e Figlio p.113. Pick up a souvenir at this long-established maker of marbled paper and notebooks.

Scuola del Cuoio p.95. Leather is a real Florentine speciality. Cross town to check out the biggest outlet for well-made and well-priced bags and belts.

🍷 **Evening around Santa Croce and Sant'Ambrogio** *Cibrèo* (p.97) is one of the best restaurants in this part of town.

Coin

San Lorenzo market

Scuola del Cuoio

Florence viewpoints

Florence is one of the most photogenic cities in Europe, and it's dotted with places that give you a great view of the townscape.

Brunelleschi's dome p.29. You could start the day by surveying the centre of the city from the summit of Brunelleschi's dome. Or, if the queue is too long, climb the adjacent Campanile instead.

Forte di Belvedere p.106. The Forte di Belvedere is open whenever it's in use as an exhibition space. If it's open when you're in town, be sure to visit – the view is terrific, and it's rarely as busy as Piazzale Michelangelo, a well-known vantage point on the neighbouring hill.

Villa Bardini p.111. The Villa Bardini often has excellent exhibitions, and the tiny third-floor terrace gives you an unforgettable panorama.

Lunch p.114 & 115. Stop for a light lunch – and a glass of fine wine – at Fuori Porta or Le Volpi e l'Uva.

Fiesole p.124. In the afternoon take a bus up to the hilltop village of Fiesole. It's an attractive little place, and the whole of Florence is spread out below.

Dinner p.127. At the end of the day, eat at La Reggia degli Etruschi or Terrazza 45, and watch the sun go down over the city.

View from the Villa Bardini

Fiesole

Le Volpi el l'Uva

Florence galleries

Of course you'll want to visit the big museums and galleries, but try to make time for some of the smaller and quirkier collections.

La Specola p.107. This is the oddest museum in the city – a collection of anatomical waxworks of dazzling accuracy and gruesome beauty.

The Museo Stefano Bardini p.110. The private art collection of Stefano Bardini, housed in the vast rooms of his former home, is displayed more or less as he left it.

The Museo Horne p.93. On the other side of the river, the collection of Herbert Percy Horne is displayed in a lovely old house that's a delight in itself.

Museo Marino Marini

🍽️ **Lunch p.98.** Have lunch at the ever-popular Osteria de' Benci, round the corner from the Horne museum, or at one of the host of other restaurants around Santa Croce.

The Museo dell'Opificio delle Pietre Dure p.79. The art of stone inlay is a Florentine speciality – the objects are not to everyone's taste, but the skill involved in their creation is astonishing.

The Museo Marino Marini p.61. A large and well-displayed collection of work by one of Italy's best-known modern artists – plus Alberti's exquisite Ruccellai chapel.

La Specola

🍷 **Drinks p.68 & 53.** After an aperitivo at the Art Bar, treat yourself to a meal at Ora d'Aria, one of the city's best restaurants.

Art Bar

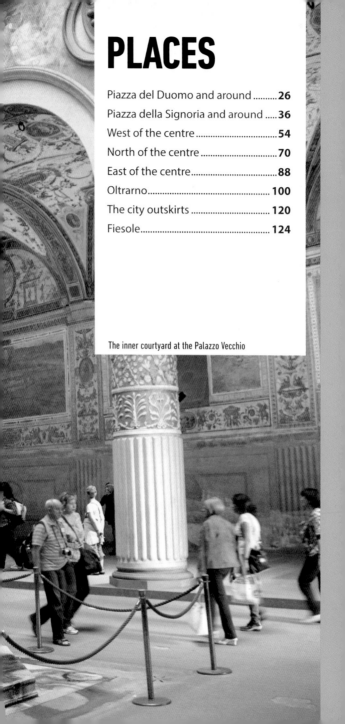

PLACES

Piazza del Duomo and around **26**

Piazza della Signoria and around **36**

West of the centre **54**

North of the centre **70**

East of the centre....................................**88**

Oltrarno.. **100**

The city outskirts **120**

Fiesole.. **124**

The inner courtyard at the Palazzo Vecchio

Piazza del Duomo and around

All first-time visitors gravitate towards Piazza del Duomo, beckoned by the pinnacle of Brunelleschi's dome, which lords it over the cityscape with an authority unmatched by any architectural creation in any other Italian city. Yet even though the magnitude of the Duomo is apparent from a distance, the first sight of the cathedral and the adjacent Baptistery still comes as a jolt, their colourful patterned exteriors making a startling contrast with the dun-toned buildings around.

Once you've finished exploring these mighty monuments, the obvious next step is to visit the superb Museo dell'Opera del Duomo, a vast repository for works of art removed over the centuries from the Duomo, Baptistery and Campanile.

The Duomo

MAP p.28, POCKET MAP C10–D10
Piazza del Duomo Ⓦ operaduomo.firenze.it.
Mon–Wed & Fri 10am–5pm, Thurs 10am–4.30pm, Sat 10am–4.45pm, Sun 1.30–4.45pm. Free.

Some time in the seventh century the seat of the Bishop of Florence was transferred from San Lorenzo to Santa Reparata, a sixth-century church which stood on the site of the present-day Duomo, or **Santa Maria del Fiore** to give it its full name. Later generations modified this older church until 1294, when Arnolfo di Cambio drafted a scheme to create the largest church in the

View from the Campanile of the Duomo

Il Grande Museo del Duomo

The major sights of Piazza del Duomo are marketed as Il Grande Museo del Duomo (W ilgrandemuseodelduomo.it). Under this scheme, a €15 ticket, valid for 48hr, gives a single admission to the Dome, the Campanile, Santa Reparata, the Museo dell'Opera del Duomo and the Baptistery; the ticket can be bought from the first three of these sights, and at a ticket office at Piazza San Giovanni 7, opposite the north doors of the Baptistery.

Catholic world. Progress on the project faltered after Arnolfo's death in 1302, but by 1418 only the dome – no small matter – remained unfinished.

Parts of the Duomo's **exterior** date back to Arnolfo's era, but most of the overblown main facade is a nineteenth-century pseudo-Gothic front. The most attractive external feature is the **Porta della Mandorla** on the north side. This doorway takes its name from the almond-shaped frame (or *mandorla*) that contains *The Assumption of the Virgin* (1414–21), sculpted by Nanni di Banco.

The Duomo's **interior** is a vast, uncluttered enclosure of bare masonry, alleviated by a pair of frescoed memorials to *condottieri* (mercenary commanders) on the north side of the nave: Paolo Uccello's monument to Sir John Hawkwood, created in 1436, and Andrea del Castagno's monument to Niccolò da Tolentino, painted twenty years later. Just beyond the horsemen, Domenico di Michelino's 1465 *Dante Explaining the Divine Comedy* gives Brunelleschi's dome – then nearing completion – a place only marginally less prominent than the mountain of Purgatory.

Barriers usually prevent visitors from going any further, but you might be able to take a look into the **Sagrestia Nuova**, where the lavish panelling is inlaid with beautiful intarsia work (1436–45) by Benedetto and Giuliano Maiano. The mighty sacristy door (1445–69), created in conjunction with Michelozzo, was Luca della Robbia's only work in bronze. It was in this sacristy that Lorenzo de' Medici took refuge in 1478 after his brother Giuliano had been mortally stabbed on the altar steps by the Pazzi conspirators (see box, p.30); the bulk of the recently installed doors protected him from his would-be assassins. Small portraits on the handles commemorate the brothers.

In the 1960s, remnants of the Duomo's predecessor, **Santa Reparata** (same hours as Duomo, except closed Sun; Il Grande Museo del Duomo ticket), were uncovered underneath the west end of the nave. Subsequent diggings have revealed a jigsaw of Roman, Paleochristian and Romanesque remains, plus fragments of mosaic and fourteenth-century frescoes and Brunelleschi's tomb, a marble slab so unassuming that it had lain forgotten under the south aisle.

Climbing the **dome** (Mon–Fri 8.30am–8pm, Sat 8.30am–5.40pm, Sun 1–4pm; Il Grande Museo del Duomo ticket; visits are timed and must be booked in advance) is an amazing experience, both for the views from the top and for the insights it offers into Brunelleschi's engineering genius (see box, p.29). Be prepared to queue, and be ready for the 463 lung-busting steps.

Piazza del Duomo and around

HOTELS AND RESIDENZE	
Bavaria	10
Benivieni	5
Brunelleschi	8
Helvetia & Bristol	9
Il Salotto di Firenze	4
Maxim	7
Novecento	3
Residenza dei Pucci	1
Savoy	6
HOSTEL	
Academy Hostel	2

CAFÉ	
Caffè Gilli	2
RESTAURANT	
Fiaschetteria Nuvoli	1

SHOPS	
Feltrinelli Red	3
IBS.it	1
Luisa at Via Roma	2
Rinascente	4

The Campanile

The Campanile

MAP p.28, POCKET MAP C10
Piazza del Duomo ⓦ operaduomo.firenze.it.
Daily 8.30am–8pm. Il Grande Museo del
Duomo ticket (see box, p.27).

The Campanile was begun in
1334 by Giotto during his period
as official city architect and *capo
maestro* (head of works) in charge
of the Duomo. By the time of his
death three years later, the base,
the first of five eventual levels,
had been completed. Andrea
Pisano, fresh from creating the
Baptistery's south doors (see p.30),
continued construction of the
second storey (1337–42), probably
in accordance with Giotto's
plans. Work was rounded off by
Francesco Talenti, who rectified
deficiencies in Giotto's original
calculations in the process: the
base's original walls teetered on
the brink of collapse until he
doubled their thickness. When
completed, the bell tower reached

84.7m, well over the limit set by the city in 1324 for civic towers.

The tower's decorative **sculptures and reliefs** – they are copies; the originals are in the Museo dell'Opera del Duomo (see p.32) – illustrate humanity's progress from original sin to a state of divine grace, a progress facilitated by manual labour, the arts and the sacraments, and guided by the influence of the planets and the cardinal and theological virtues.

A climb to the summit is one of the highlights of any Florentine trip: the parapet at the top of the tower is a less lofty but in many ways more satisfying viewpoint than the cathedral dome, if only because the view takes in the dome itself. There are 414 steps to the summit – and there's no lift.

The Duomo's dome

Brunelleschi's dome

Since Arnolfo di Cambio's model of the Duomo collapsed some time in the fourteenth century, nobody has been sure quite how he intended to crown his achievement. In 1367 Neri di Fioraventi proposed the construction of a magnificent cupola that was to span nearly 43m, broader than the dome of Rome's Pantheon, which had been the world's largest for 1300 years.

There was just one problem: nobody had worked out how to build such a thing. Medieval arches were usually built on wooden "centring", a network of timbers that held the stone in place until the mortar was set. In the case of the Duomo, the weight of the stone would have been too great for the timber. Eventually the project was thrown open to competition, and a goldsmith and clockmaker, Filippo Brunelleschi, presented the winning scheme. The key to Brunelleschi's success lay in the construction of the dome as two masonry shells, each built as a stack of ever-diminishing rings. Secured with hidden stone beams and enormous iron chains, these concentric circles formed a lattice that was filled with lightweight bricks laid in a herringbone pattern that prevented the higher sections from falling inwards.

The dome's completion was marked by the consecration of the cathedral on March 25, 1436 – Annunciation Day, and the Florentine New Year – in a ceremony conducted by the pope. Even then, the topmost piece, the lantern, remained unfinished, with many people convinced the dome could support no further weight. But once again Brunelleschi won the day, beginning work on the dome's final stage in 1446, just a few months before his death. The whole thing was finally completed in the late 1460s, when the cross and gilded ball, both cast by Verrocchio, were hoisted into place. It is still the largest masonry dome in the world.

The Baptistery

MAP p.28, POCKET MAP C10
Piazza del Duomo Ⓦ operaduomo.firenze.it.
Mon–Sat 8.15am–8pm, Sun & first Sat of
month 8.30am–2pm. Il Grande Museo del
Duomo ticket (see box, p.27).

Generally thought to date from the sixth or seventh century, the Baptistery is the **oldest building** in Florence, and was first documented in 897, when it was the city's cathedral.

The Florentines were always conscious of their Roman ancestry, and for centuries believed that the Baptistery was a converted Roman temple to Mars. This isn't the case, but its exterior marble cladding – applied between about 1059 and 1128 – is clearly classical in inspiration, while its most famous embellishments, the gilded **bronze doors**, mark the emergence of a more scholarly, self-conscious interest in the art of the ancient world.

The arrival of Andrea Pisano in Florence in 1330 offered the chance to outdo the celebrated bronze portals of archrival Pisa's cathedral. Most of the **south doors'** 28 panels, installed in 1339, form a narrative on the life of St John the Baptist, patron saint of Florence and the Baptistery's dedicatee.

Some sixty years of financial and political turmoil, and the ravages of the Black Death, prevented further work on the Baptistery's other entrances until 1401. That year a competition was held to design a

The Pazzi Conspiracy

The Pazzi Conspiracy had its roots in the election in 1472 of Pope Sixtus IV, who promptly made six of his nephews cardinals. One of them, Girolamo Riario, received particularly preferential treatment, probably because he was in fact Sixtus's son. Sixtus's plan was that Riario should take over the town of Imola as a base for papal expansion, and accordingly he approached Lorenzo de' Medici for the necessary loan. When Lorenzo rebuffed him, and in addition refused to recognize Francesco Salviati as archbishop of Pisa, a furious Sixtus turned to the Pazzi, the Medici's leading Florentine rivals as bankers in Rome.

Three co-conspirators met in Rome in the early months of 1477: Riario, now in possession of Imola but eager for greater spoils; Salviati, incandescent at Lorenzo's veto; and Francesco de' Pazzi, head of the Pazzi's Rome operation and determined to usurp Medici power in Florence. After numerous false starts, it was decided to murder Lorenzo and Giuliano while they attended Mass in Florence's cathedral. The date set was Sunday, April 26, 1478: Lorenzo's extermination was delegated to two embittered priests, Maffei and Bagnone, whereas Giuliano was to be dispatched by Francesco de' Pazzi and Bernardo Baroncelli, a Pazzi sidekick.

It all went horribly wrong. Giuliano was killed, but Lorenzo managed to escape, fleeing wounded to the Duomo's new sacristy. The conspirators were soon dealt with: Salviati and Francesco de' Pazzi were hanged from a window of the Palazzo della Signoria; Maffei and Bagnone were castrated and hanged; Baroncelli escaped to Constantinople but was extradited and executed; and Jacopo de' Pazzi, the godfather of the Pazzi clan, was tortured, hanged alongside the decomposing Salviati and finally hurled into the river.

new set of doors, with the entrants being asked to create a panel showing the Sacrifice of Isaac. The judges found themselves equally impressed by the work of two young goldsmiths, **Brunelleschi** and **Lorenzo Ghiberti**; both winning entries are displayed in the Bargello (see p.46). Unable to choose between the pair, the judges suggested that they work in tandem. Brunelleschi replied that if he couldn't do the job alone he wasn't interested – whereupon the contract was handed to Ghiberti.

His **north doors** (1403–24) show a new naturalism and classicized sense of composition, but they are as nothing to the gilded **east doors** (1425–52), which have long been known as the "Gates of Paradise", supposedly because Michelangelo once remarked that they were so beautiful they deserved to be the portals of heaven. These are copies – the originals are in the Museo dell'Opera del Duomo (see p.32).

The Baptistery **interior** is stunning, with its black and white marble cladding and miscellany of ancient columns below a blazing thirteenth-century mosaic ceiling, dominated by Christ in Judgement. The interior's semi-abstract mosaic pavement also

The Baptistery

dates from the thirteenth century. The empty octagon at its centre marks the spot once occupied by the huge font in which every child born in the city during the previous twelve months would be baptized on March 25 (New Year's Day in the old Florentine calendar). To the right of the altar lies the tomb of Baldassare Cossa, the schismatic Pope John XXIII, who was deposed in 1415 and died in Florence in 1419.

The ceiling of the Baptistery

The Museo dell'Opera del Duomo

MAP p.28, POCKET MAP D10
Piazza del Duomo ⓦ ilgrandemuseodel
duomo.it. Daily 9am–8pm; closed 1st Tues
of month. Il Grande Museo del Duomo
ticket (see box, p.27).

In 1296 a body called the Opera del Duomo ("Work of the Duomo") was created to oversee the maintenance of the Duomo. Since the early fifteenth century its home has been the building behind the east end of the cathedral at Piazza del Duomo 9, which also houses the superb Museo dell'Opera del Duomo.

Reopened in late 2015, after a €50 million rebuild that extended the museum into an adjacent eighteenth-century theatre, the collection comprises more than 750 items, arrayed over three floors. The show-stopper on the ground floor is a huge top-lit hall containing a reconstruction of **Arnolfo di Cambio**'s facade of the Duomo. Nearly 40m wide and 20m tall, the replica is adorned with many of the sculptures that occupied the facade's various niches before it was dismantled in 1587. Arnolfo and his workshop produced the eerily glass-eyed *Madonna and Child*; equally striking are his *St Reparata*, one of Florence's patron saints, and the ramrod-straight statue of Boniface VIII, whose corruption earned him a place in Dante's *Inferno*, which was partly written during Boniface's pontificate. Of the four seated figures of the Evangelists, Nanni di Banco's *St Luke* and Donatello's *St John* are particularly fine. Facing the facade are **Ghiberti**'s stupendous gilded bronze "Doors of Paradise" and the Baptistery's original North Doors, also created by Ghiberti. These will soon be joined by the originals of Andrea Pisano's South Doors.

Also on the ground floor you'll find a room devoted to **Michelangelo**'s anguished *Pietà* (1550–53), which was removed from the cathedral in 1981. Carved when he was almost 80, this is one of his last works, and was intended for his own tomb; Vasari records that the face of Nicodemus is a self-portrait. Dissatisfied with the quality of the marble, Michelangelo mutilated the group by hammering off the left leg and arm of Christ; a pupil restored the arm, then finished off the figure of Mary Magdalene.

In the adjacent room the greatest of Michelangelo's precursors, **Donatello**, provides the focus with a gaunt wooden figure of Mary Magdalene (1453–55), created for the Baptistery. The adjoining octagonal chapel features an assembly of reliquaries which contain, among other saintly remains, the jaw of Saint Jerome and an index finger of John the Baptist.

The Museo dell'Opera del Duomo

Donatello's *Cantoria*

There are more masterpieces by Donatello upstairs, where the long Galleria del Campanile – which overlooks the di Cambio facade – is lined with sixteen life-sized sculptures and 54 bas-relief panels from the Campanile. Five of the large figures are by Donatello, with perhaps the most powerful of them being the prophet Habbakuk, the intensity of whose gaze is said to have prompted the sculptor to seize it and yell, "Speak, speak!" Keeping company with Donatello's work are four Prophets (1348–50) and two Sibyls (1342–48) attributed to Andrea Pisano, and *The Sacrifice of Isaac* (1421), a collaboration between Nanni di Bartolo and Donatello. The gallery's bas-reliefs depict the spiritual refinement of humanity through labour, the arts and, ultimately, the virtues and sacraments. The key panels are the hexagonal reliefs from the lower tier, all of which – save for the last five, by Luca della Robbia (1437–39) – were the work of **Andrea Pisano** and his son Nino (c.1348–50), probably to designs by Giotto.

Donatello's magnificent *cantoria*, or choir loft (1433–39), with its playground of boisterous putti, hangs on the wall of another spectacular room; on the opposite wall is the *cantoria* created by the young Luca della Robbia (the original panels are displayed below the *cantoria*, with casts replacing them in the loft itself). In the Sala del Tesoro you'll find an amazing **silver altar-front** that's covered with scenes from the life of St John the Baptist. Begun in 1366, this mighty piece was completed in 1480, the culmination of a century of labour by, among others, Michelozzo, Antonio del Pollaiuolo and Verrocchio. Next door there's a sequence of marble reliefs by Bacio Bandinelli and Giovanni Bandini, part of an unfinished sequence of three hundred panels proposed for the cathedral choir.

On the top floor are displayed designs for the Duomo's facade. The itinerary ends on a panoramic terrace offering a terrific view of Brunelleschi's dome.

Florence – the capital of Italy

At the start of 1865 Florence became the first capital of the newly united Italy. It was to hold this position for only five years, but during this period a transformation of the city was begun, following a plan conceived by Giuseppe Poggi (1811–1901). The city walls were demolished, and wide boulevards or *viali* put in their place; shopping streets such as Via de' Cerretani and Via de' Tornabuoni were widened and modernized; the riverbanks were developed; and Piazzale Michelangelo was created on the hill of San Miniato. But the most drastic intervention in the city centre was the removal of the old market and the surrounding slums – a new market hall was built near San Lorenzo, and the ancient market area became Piazza della Repubblica.

Piazza della Repubblica

MAP p.28, POCKET MAP B11

A short distance to the south of Piazza del Duomo, the vacant expanse of Piazza della Repubblica opens up. Impressive solely for its size, this square was planned in the late 1860s, as part of Giuseppe Poggi's masterplan for the capital of the recently formed Italian nation. However, the clearance of the **Mercato Vecchio** had not even begun when the capital was transferred to Rome, and it wasn't until 1885 that the marketplace and its disease-ridden tenements were finally swept away. On the west side a vast **arch** bears the

triumphant inscription: "The ancient city centre restored to new life from the squalor of centuries."

The free standing column is the solitary trace of the piazza's history. Once surrounded by stalls, it used to be topped by Donatello's statue of Abundance, and a bell that was rung to signal the start and close of trading. Nowadays, Piazza della Repubblica is best known for the three large and expensive **cafés** that stand on the perimeter: the *Gilli* (see p.35); the *Giubbe Rosse*, where the Futurist manifesto was launched in 1909; and the *Paszkowski*, which began business as a beer hall in the 1840s.

Piazza della Repubblica

Shops

Feltrinelli Red

MAP p.28, POCKET MAP B11
Piazza della Repubblica 27r ☎ 055 213
110, ⓦ lafeltrinelli.it. Daily 9am–11pm.

The Feltrinelli Red format
– combining a multi-floor
bookshop with a caffè-restaurant
(*Red* stands for "read, eat,
dream") – was pioneered in
Rome and has now come to
Florence, taking over what was
formerly the Edison megastore.
The stock is more impressive,
though, at the city's other
Feltrinelli branch, at Via de'
Cerretani 30r nearby.

IBS.it

MAP p.28, POCKET MAP B10
Via de' Cerretani 16r ☎ 055 287 339,
ⓦ ibs.it. Mon–Thurs 9am–8pm, Fri & Sat
9am–midnight, Sun 10am–8pm.

Florence's branch of the nationwide
IBS is the biggest bookshop in
the city.

Luisa at Via Roma

MAP p.28, POCKET MAP B10
Via Roma 19–21r ☎ 055 217 826,
ⓦ luisaviaroma.com. Mon–Sat
10.30am–7.30pm, Sun 11am–7.30pm.

Luisa was founded back in the
1930s and remains Florence's top-
end multi-label clothes shop. The
interior is one of Florence's more
impressive examples of modern
architectural design.

Rinascente

MAP p.28, POCKET MAP C11
Piazza della Repubblica 1 ☎ 055 239 8544,
ⓦ rinascente.it. Mon–Fri 9.30am–8.30pm,
Sat 9am–9pm, Sun 10.30am–8pm.

Like Coin (see p.51), Rinascente
is part of a countrywide chain,
though this store, opened in 1996,
is a touch more upmarket than its
nearby rival, and bigger, with six
floors of clothes, linen, cosmetics,
and other household stuff. The
rooftop café gives a great view of
the Duomo.

Cantucci at Caffè Gilli

Café

Caffè Gilli

MAP p.28, POCKET MAP B11
Via Roma 1r ☎ 055 213 896, ⓦ gilli.it.
Daily 7.30am–midnight.

This is the most appealing
of Piazza della Repubblica's
expensive cafés. It was founded in
1733 and has a lavish belle époque
interior. On a cold afternoon try
the famous hot chocolate, which
comes in five blended flavours.

Restaurant

Fiaschetteria Nuvoli

MAP p.28, POCKET MAP B10
Piazza dell'Olio 15 ☎ 055 239 6616.
Mon–Sat noon–9pm.

For a basic meal within a stone's
throw of the Duomo, you can't
do better than this. Upstairs,
the tiny, dark, bottle-lined bar
is dominated by a counter laden
with cold meats, *crostini* and other
snacks. In the basement, good-
value Florentine staples are served
at half a dozen communal tables.

Piazza della Signoria and around

Whereas the Piazza del Duomo provides the focus for the city's religious life, the Piazza della Signoria – site of the magnificent Palazzo Vecchio and forecourt to the Uffizi gallery – has always been the centre of its secular existence. Created in 1307, to provide a setting for the Palazzo Vecchio, the piazza was paved by 1385 and reached its present-day dimensions in 1871, after Florence's brief spell as the capital of the country.

The dense network of streets northeast of the Piazza della Signoria is dominated by the campanile of the Badìa Fiorentina, the most important of several buildings in the area that have the strongest associations with Dante Alighieri. Immediately opposite the church stands the forbidding bulk of the Bargello, once the city's prison, now home to a superb collection of sculpture and objets d'art. To the south of the Bargello, at the back of the Uffizi, lies the fascinating Museo Galileo, a sight too often overlooked by art-obsessed visitors.

The main catwalk of the Florentine passeggiata is Via dei Calzaiuoli, the broad avenue that links Piazza della Signoria with Piazza del Duomo. Shop-lined for most of its length, it boasts one stupendous monument, the church of Orsanmichele.

The Piazza della Signoria statues

MAP p.38, POCKET MAP C12

Florence's political volatility is encapsulated by the Piazza della Signoria's array of **statues**. From left to right, the line-up starts with Giambologna's equestrian statue (1587–94) of Cosimo I; mimicking the famous Marcus Aurelius statue in Rome, it was designed to draw parallels between the power of medieval Florence (and thus Cosimo) and the glory of imperial Rome.

Next comes Ammannati's fatuous **Neptune** fountain (1565–75), a tribute to Cosimo's prowess as a naval commander. Neptune himself is a lumpen lout of a figure, who provoked Michelangelo to coin the rhyming put-down *Ammannato, Ammannato, che bel marmo hai rovinato* ("…what a fine piece of marble you've ruined"). After a copy of Donatello's *Marzocco* (1418–20), the original of which is in the Bargello, comes a replica of the same sculptor's *Judith and Holofernes* (1456–60), which freezes the action at the moment Judith's arm begins its scything stroke – a dramatic conception that no other sculptor of the period would have attempted. Commissioned by Cosimo de'

The Neptune fountain, Piazza della Signoria

Medici, this statue doubled as a fountain in the Palazzo Medici but was removed to the Piazza della Signoria after the expulsion of the family in 1495, to be displayed as an emblem of vanquished tyranny; the original is in the Palazzo Vecchio.

Michelangelo's **David**, at first intended for the Duomo, was also installed here in 1504 as a declaration of civic solidarity by the Florentine Republic; the original is now cooped up in the Accademia (see p.78). Bandinelli's adjacent *Hercules and Cacus* (1534) was designed as a personal emblem of Cosimo I and a symbol of Florentine fortitude. Benvenuto Cellini described the muscle-bound Hercules as looking like "a sackful of melons".

The Loggia della Signoria

MAP p.38, POCKET MAP C12–C13

The square's grace note, the Loggia della Signoria, was completed in 1382 and served as a dais for city dignitaries, a forum for meeting foreign emissaries and a platform for the swearing-in of public officials. Its alternative name, the Loggia dei Lanzi, comes from Cosimo I's bodyguard of Swiss lancers, who were garrisoned nearby.

Although Donatello's *Judith and Holofernes* was placed here as early as 1506, it was only in the late eighteenth century that the loggia became exclusively a **showcase** for sculpture. In the corner nearest the Palazzo Vecchio stands a figure that has become one of the iconic images of the Renaissance, Benvenuto Cellini's *Perseus* (1554). Made for Cosimo I, the statue symbolizes the triumph of firm grand ducal rule over the monstrous indiscipline of all other forms of government. Equally attention-seeking is Giambologna's last work, to the right, *The Rape of the Sabine* (1583), the epitome of the Mannerist obsession with spiralling forms. The sculptor intended the piece merely as a study of old age, male strength and female beauty; the present name was coined after the event. The figures along the back wall are Roman works, traditionally believed to portray empresses, while of the three central statues only one – Giambologna's *Hercules Slaying the Centaur* (1599) – deserves such prominence.

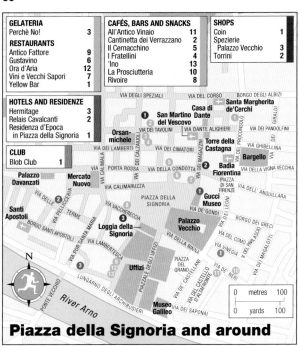

GELATERIA		CAFÉS, BARS AND SNACKS		SHOPS	
Perchè No!	3	All'Antico Vinaio	11	Coin	1
RESTAURANTS		Cantinetta dei Verrazzano	2	Spezierie	
Antico Fattore	9	Il Cernacchino	5	Palazzo Vecchio	3
Gustavino	6	I Fratellini	4	Torrini	2
Ora d'Aria	12	'Ino	13		
Vini e Vecchi Sapori	7	La Prosciutteria	10		
Yellow Bar	1	Rivoire	8		

HOTELS AND RESIDENZE	
Hermitage	3
Relais Cavalcanti	2
Residenza d'Epoca in Piazza della Signoria	1

CLUB	
Blob Club	1

Piazza della Signoria and around

Cosimo I in front of the Gucci Museo

Gucci Museo

MAP p.38, POCKET MAP D12
Piazza della Signoria 10. Ⓦ guccimuseo.com.
Daily 10am–8pm. €7.

The piazza's massive fourteenth-century Palazzo della Mercanzia now houses the Gucci Museo, a temple to Florence's most famous **fashion house**. Founded by Guccio Gucci in 1921, the company lost its way in the 1980s and the family was forced to sell to a Bahraini investment group. Rescued by the US designer Tom Ford, Gucci is once again one of Italy's coolest labels. As you'd expect, there are some fabulous clothes here, plus a plethora of ridiculous items, such as Gucci-monogrammed scuba flippers. Contemporary art from the vast collection of François-Henri Pinault, boss of the company that owns Gucci, is also on show; there's a café and gift shop too, in case you want to drop a couple of hundred euros on a Gucci belt.

The Florentine Republic

Between 1293 and 1534 – bar the odd ruction – Florence maintained a republican constitution that was embodied in well-defined institutions. The rulers were drawn from the ranks of guild members over the age of 30, and were chosen in a public ceremony held every two months. At this ceremony, eight men were picked by lottery to become the *Priori* (or *Signori*), forming a government called the *Signoria*. Once elected, the *Priori* moved into the Palazzo della Signoria, where they stayed throughout their brief period of office.

Headed by the *Gonfaloniere* (the "Standard-Bearer"), the *Signoria* consulted two elected councils, or *Collegi*, as well as committees introduced to deal with specific crises. Permanent officials included the Chancellor (a post once held by Machiavelli) and the *Podestà*, a magistrate brought in from a neighbouring city as an independent arbitrator. In times of extreme crisis all male citizens over the age of 14 (apart from clerics) were summoned to a *Parlamento* in Piazza della Signoria. When a two-thirds quorum was reached, the people were asked to approve a *Balìa*, a committee to deal with the situation as it saw fit.

All this looked good on paper, but political cliques had few problems ensuring that only likely supporters found their way into the lottery process. If a rogue candidate slipped through the net, or things went awry, then a *Parlamento* was summoned, and the resulting *Balìa* replaced the offending person with a more pliable candidate. It was by such means that the mercantile dynasties – the Peruzzi, the Albizzi, the Strozzi and of course the Medici – retained their power even when not technically in office.

The Siege of Florence in The Palazzo Vecchio

The Palazzo Vecchio

MAP p.38, POCKET MAP C12–D13
Piazza della Signoria
ⓦ museicivicifiorentini.comune.fi.it.
April–Sept Mon–Wed & Fri–Sun 9am–11pm
(tower closes at 9pm), Thurs closes 2pm;
Oct–March Mon–Wed & Fri–Sun 9am–7pm
(tower closes at 5pm), Thurs closes 2pm.
€10, or €14 with tower; €4 guided tour of
excavations (children not permitted).

Florence's fortress-like **town hall**, the Palazzo Vecchio, was begun in the last year of the thirteenth century, as the home of the *Priori*, or *Signoria*, the highest tier of the city's republican government (see box, p.39). In 1540 Cosimo I moved his retinue here from the Palazzo Medici and grafted a huge extension onto the rear of the building. The Medici remained in residence for only nine years before moving to the Palazzo Pitti – that's when the "old" (*vecchio*) palace acquired its present name.

The small – and free – **Tracce di Firenze** (Traces of Florence) museum, on the ground floor of the palazzo, is in essence a collection of maps, prints, photos and topographical paintings that

The Palazzo Vecchio

chart the growth of Florence from the fifteenth century to the present. Perhaps the most impressive item is the meticulous nineteenth-century reproduction of a 1472 aerial view of Florence called the **Pianta della Catena** (Chain Map), the original of which was destroyed in Berlin during World War II.

Work on the beautiful inner **courtyard** was begun by Michelozzo in 1453; the decoration was largely added by Vasari on the occasion of Francesco de' Medici's marriage to Johanna of Austria in 1565.

Vasari was given full rein in the huge **Salone del Cinquecento** at the top of the stairs. The chamber might have had one of Italy's most remarkable decorative schemes: Leonardo da Vinci and Michelangelo were employed to paint frescoes on opposite sides of the room, but Leonardo's work, *The Battle of Anghiari*, was abandoned after his experimental technique went wrong, while Michelangelo's *The Battle of Cascina* had not left the drawing board when he was summoned to Rome by Pope Julius II in 1506. Instead, the hall received six drearily bombastic murals (1563–65) – painted either by Vasari or under his direction – illustrating Florentine military triumphs over Pisa and Siena. It has generally been assumed that Vasari obliterated whatever remained of Leonardo's fresco before beginning his work, but the discovery of a cavity behind *The Battle of Marciano* has raised the possibility that Vasari instead constructed a false wall for his fresco, to preserve his great predecessor's painting. Investigations are proceeding.

The **sculptural highlight** is Michelangelo's *Victory*, almost opposite the entrance door. Carved for the tomb of Pope Julius II, the statue was donated to the

Medici by the artist's nephew, then installed here by Vasari in 1565 to celebrate Cosimo's defeat of the Sienese ten years earlier. Directly opposite is the plaster model of a companion piece for the *Victory*, Giambologna's *Virtue Overcoming Vice*, another metaphor for Florentine military might.

From the Salone del Cinquecento, a roped-off door allows a glimpse of the most bizarre room in the building, the **Studiolo di Francesco I**. Designed by Vasari and decorated by no fewer than thirty Mannerist artists (1570–74), this windowless cell was created as a retreat for the introverted son of Cosimo and Eleanor, whose portraits face each other across the room.

Upstairs, in the six rooms of the Quartiere di Eleonora di Toledo, the star turn is the tiny and exquisite **Cappella di Eleonora**, vividly decorated in glassy Mannerist style by Bronzino in the 1540s. The **Sala dell'Udienza**, which was originally the audience chamber of the Republic, boasts a stunning gilt-coffered ceiling by Giuliano da Maiano, who was also responsible, with his brother Benedetto, for the intarsia work on the doors and the lovely doorway that leads into the **Sala dei Gigli**, a room that takes its name from the lilies (*gigli*) that adorn most of its surfaces. The room has another splendid ceiling by the Maiano brothers, and a fresco by Domenico Ghirlandaio of *SS Zenobius, Stephen and Lorenzo* (1481–85),

Cappella di Eleonora

but the undoubted highlight here is Donatello's original *Judith and Holofernes* (1455–60).

Outside the Sala dei Gigli, a staircase leads to the **tower** of the Palazzo Vecchio (€10, or €14 with the Palazzo Vecchio); a 223-step climb takes you to a terrace beneath the bell chambers, passing the prison cell known ironically as the Alberghinetto (Little Hotel), where Cosimo il Vecchio and Savonarola were both held.

The palazzo was built over an amphitheatre that was raised during the reign of Emperor Hadrian. The excavated ruins are open to the public by guided tour, which must be booked when you buy a ticket.

Percorsi Segreti

The Palazzo Vecchio's **Percorsi Segreti** ("Secret Passageways") allows access – on guided tours only, of up to twelve people at a time – to parts of the building that are normally off-limits, such as the Studiolo di Francesco I and the extraordinary space between the roof and ceiling of the Salone del Cinquecento. **Tickets** cost €4, in addition to the entrance ticket for the Palazzo. The hour-long tours take place most days at 10am, 11.30am, 2.30pm & 4pm (Thurs 10am & 11.30am only) in Italian, French and English. Reserve a place when you buy your Palazzo Vecchio ticket. Minimum age is 12.

The Uffizi

MAP p.38, POCKET MAP C13
Piazzale degli Uffizi ⓦuffizi.it. Tues–Sun
8.15am–6.50pm; in summer and at festive
periods it sometimes stays open until
10pm. €20 March–Oct, €12 Nov–Feb; a
12-month pass is €50 (or €70 with Palazzo
Pitti and Boboli gardens), and there's a
€38/18 3-day pass for the Uffizi and all the
Palazzo Pitti museums plus the Boboli.

The **Galleria degli Uffizi** is housed
in what were once government
offices (*uffizi*) built by Vasari for
Cosimo I, which later became
the home of the Medici's art
collection. In the nineteenth
century a large proportion of
the statuary was transferred to
the Bargello, while most of the
antiquities went to the Museo
Archeologico, leaving the Uffizi
as essentially a stupendous gallery
of paintings supplemented with
some classical sculptures.

In the late 1990s the Uffizi began
a huge renovation and expansion
project, which has more than
doubled the exhibition space by
opening new suites of galleries on
the first floor. There's an improved
café and a huge new bookshop
too, but the so-called "Nuovo
Uffizi" was still not completely
finished when we went to press,
and the gallery seems to have
fewer staff that it needs – you
should expect to find several
rooms closed. Some rehanging is
still taking place, so some pictures
might not be exactly in the
locations given below.

The parade of masterpieces
begins immediately, with
altarpieces of the *Maestà*
(Madonna Enthroned) by **Duccio**,
Cimabue and **Giotto**. Painters
from fourteenth-century Siena
soon follow, with several pieces by
Ambrogio and Pietro Lorenzetti,
and **Simone Martini**'s glorious
Annunciation. In rooms 5–7
there's a display of paintings that
mark the summit of the precious
style known as International
Gothic; the outstanding pieces
here are **Lorenzo Monaco**'s
Coronation of the Virgin (1415)
and the *Adoration of the Magi*
(1423) by **Gentile da Fabriano**.

In **Room 8**, you'll see Fra'
Angelico's gorgeous *Coronation of
the Virgin* and **Paolo Uccello**'s *The
Battle of San Romano*, which once
hung in Lorenzo il Magnifico's
bedchamber. A lot of space in
this room is given over to **Filippo
Lippi**, whose *Madonna and Child
with Two Angels* supplies one of the
gallery's most popular faces: the
model was Lucrezia Buti, a convent
novice who became his mistress.
Lucrezia puts in an another
appearance in Lippi's *Coronation
of the Virgin*, where she's the young
woman gazing out in the right
foreground; Filippo himself, hand
on chin, makes eye contact on the
left side of the picture.

A staggering array of work by
Filippo Lippi's pupil, **Botticelli**, fills
the connected rooms 10–14. *The
Primavera* and *The Birth of Venus*
are the crowd-pullers, but don't

Uffizi practicalities

Queues for on-the-day admission to the Uffizi in high season
take hours to move, so in summer you'd be wise to pay the €4
surcharge for booking a ticket in advance. Tickets can be reserved
at the Uffizi, or at the Firenze Musei ticket booths at Orsanmichele
(Mon–Sat 9am–4.15pm) and the Libreria My Accademia, Via
Ricasoli 105r (Tues–Sun 8.15am–5pm), or by calling ☎055 294
883. Even if you have bought an advance ticket, get there half an
hour before your allotted admission time, because the queues are
often enormous. Full admission costs €20/12.

Michelangelo room in the Uffizi

overlook Botticelli's wonderful religious paintings, such as the *Madonna of the Magnificat* and the *Madonna of the Pomegranate*. Room 15, home to Botticelli's *Adoration of the Magi*, is dominated by the beautiful *Adoration of the Shepherds* by his Flemish contemporary **Hugo van der Goes**.

Beyond the octagonal **Tribuna**, which houses several items from the Medici's collection of **classical sculptures**, rooms 19–23 are devoted to non-Tuscan painters of the early Italian Renaissance. Room 20 is particularly strong, with a pair of gorgeous pictures by **Antonello da Messina**, a perplexing *Sacred Allegory* by **Giovanni Bellini**, beautiful paintings by **Cima da Conegliano** and **Carpaccio** and a stupendous array of works by **Mantegna**.

On the opposite side of the Uffizi, a room is given over to Raphael's teacher, **Perugino**, who is represented by a typically placid and contemplative *Madonna and Child with Saints* (1493), and *Pietà* (1494–95). Next comes Filippino Lippi, who shares space with **Piero di Cosimo**, creator of the bizarre *Perseus Freeing Andromeda* and *The Incarnation*. In this part of the Uffizi the biggest draw is the **Michelangelo** room, where the focal point is his *Doni Tondo*, the only easel painting he came close to completing. Works from various illustrious contemporaries of Michelangelo occupy the rest of the wall space.

Beyond the majestic **Niobe Room**, room 45 is currently being used as a sort of parking space for pictures that await a new permanent home. Downstairs, the section devoted to **non-Italian artists** has no fewer than four Rembrandt portraits; Goya, El Greco and Chardin are just a few of the other great foreigners you'll find here. Most of this floor, however, is taken up with Italian art. **Andrea del Sarto**, **Leonardo da Vinci**, **Rosso Fiorentino** and **Pontormo** are given solo rooms, while Pontormo's protegé, **Bronzino**, gets even more space. Room 66 is packed with pictures by **Raphael**, then come **Correggio** and **Parmigianino**, followed by the Venetians: room 83 is given over to **Titian**, with eleven of his paintings on show. Works by **Salvator Rosa**, **Luca Giordano** and **Artemisia Gentileschi** make a strong impact in the last rooms, where the dominant presence is **Caravaggio**.

The Corridoio Vasariano

A door on the Uffizi's west corridor, between rooms 25 and 34, opens onto the **Corridoio Vasariano**, a passageway built by Vasari in 1565 to link the Palazzo Vecchio to the Palazzo Pitti, via the Uffizi. Winding its way down to the river, over the Ponte Vecchio, through the church of Santa Felicita and into the Giardino di Boboli, it gives a fascinating series of clandestine views of the city. As if that weren't pleasure enough, the corridor is lined with paintings, the larger portion of which comprises a gallery of **self-portraits**, featuring such greats as Andrea del Sarto, Bronzino, Rubens, Velazquez, David, Delacroix and Ingres. However, there are plans to move the best of the paintings into the extended Uffizi galleries, and access to the corridor is erratic – various private companies offer visits priced in the region of €100, but the Uffizi sometimes opens the corridor for small-group guided tours by Uffizi staff, usually in Italian only. For the latest situation, ask at the Amici degli Uffizi office at the Uffizi or at one of the tourist offices.

The Museo Galileo

MAP p.38, POCKET MAP C13
Piazza dei Giudici 1 Ⓦ museogalileo.it.
Mon & Wed–Sun 9.30am–6pm, Tues
9.30am–1pm. €9.

Long after Florence had declined from its artistic apogee, the intellectual reputation of the city was maintained by its scientists, many of them directly encouraged

Armillary sphere in the Museo Galileo

by the ruling Medici-Lorraine dynasty. Two of the latter, Grand Duke Ferdinando II and his brother Leopoldo, both of whom studied with Galileo, founded a scientific academy at the Pitti in 1657. Called the Accademia del Cimento (Academy of Experiment), its motto was "Try and try again." The instruments made and acquired by this academy are the core of the city's science museum, recently rebranded as the Museo Galileo.

Some of Galileo's original instruments are on show on the first floor, such as the telescope with which he discovered the four moons of Jupiter, which he tactfully named the Medicean planets. On this floor you'll also find the museum's holy relics – bones from three of Galileo's fingers, plus a tooth. Other cases are filled with beautiful Arab astrolabes, calculating machines, early telescopes, and some delicate and ornate thermometers. The most imposing single exhibit on this floor is a massive armillary sphere made in 1593 for Ferdinando I to provide a visual proof of the supposed veracity of the earth-centred Ptolemaic system.

On the floor above there are all kinds of exquisitely manufactured scientific and mechanical equipment, several built to demonstrate the fundamental laws of physics. Dozens of clocks and timepieces are on show too, along with some spectacular electrical machines, cases of alarming surgical instruments, and anatomical wax models for teaching obstetrics.

On the ground floor, on your way out, you'll go through a new interactive area that explicates the principles underlying some of the exhibits upstairs; video screens in some of the upper rooms do a similar job.

The Badìa Fiorentina

MAP p.38, POCKET MAP D12
Via del Proconsolo. Open to tourists Mon 3–6pm. €3.

The Badìa Fiorentina, one of the most impressive churches in the centre of the city, was founded in 978 by Willa, widow of the Margrave of Tuscany, in honour of her husband, and it became one of the focal buildings in medieval Florence. The city's sick were treated in a hospital founded here in 1031, while the main bell marked the divisions of the working day. It was chosen as the venue for Boccaccio's celebrated lectures on Dante, which the city authorities commissioned in 1373.

The Badìa's hospital owed much to Willa's son, Ugo, who further endowed his mother's foundation after a vision of hellish torments. The 1280s saw the church overhauled, and later Baroque additions smothered much of the old church, though the narrow campanile escaped unharmed. Completed around 1330, it remains a prominent feature of the Florentine skyline.

Inside the church you'll find the tomb monument to Ugo, sculpted by Mino da Fiesole between 1469 and 1481. The other outstanding

The Badìa Fiorentina

work of art is Filippino Lippi's superb *Apparition of the Virgin to St Bernard* (c.1485), in which Bernard is shown in the act of writing a homily aimed at those caught between the "rocks" of tribulation and the "chains" of sin; the presence of the four monks reinforces the message that redemption lies in the contemplative life.

Nowadays the Badìa belongs to the Fraternity of Jerusalem, a French monastic order founded in the 1970s, which allows tourists to peep into the church whenever a service isn't in progress. Only on Monday afternoons, however, are visitors allowed to see the upper storey of the **Chiostro degli Aranci** (Cloister of the Oranges), which is named after the fruit trees that used to be grown here. Two of its flanks are graced with an anonymous but highly distinctive fresco cycle (1436–39) on the life of St Benedict. A later panel, showing the saint throwing himself into bushes to resist temptation, is by the young Bronzino.

The courtyard of the Bargello

The Bargello

MAP p.38, POCKET MAP D12
Via del Proconsolo 4 ⓦ uffizi.firenze.it.
Tues–Sat 8.15am–2pm, plus second &
fourth Mon of month and first, and third &
fifth Sun of month, same hours, with
longer hours (and higher admission
charge) for special exhibitions. €8.

The Museo Nazionale del Bargello
occupies the dour Palazzo del
Bargello, which was built in 1255
and soon became the seat of the
Podestà, the city's chief magistrate,
and the site of the main law court.
The building acquired its present
name after 1574, when the Medici
abolished the post of *Podestà* and
the building became home to the
chief of police – the *Bargello*.

You've no time to catch your
breath in the Bargello: the
room immediately behind the
ticket office is crammed with
treasures, chief of which are
the work of **Michelangelo**, in
whose shadow every Florentine
sculptor laboured.

The tipsy, soft-bellied figure of
Bacchus (1496–97) was his first
major sculpture, carved at the age
of 22, a year or so before his great
Pietà in Rome. Michelangelo's
style soon evolved into something
less ostentatiously virtuosic, as
is shown by the tender *Tondo
Pitti* (1503–05), while the rugged
expressivity of his late manner
is exemplified by the square-
jawed *Bust of Brutus* (c.1540),
the artist's sole work of this kind.
A powerful portrait sketch in
stone, it's a coded celebration of
anti-Medicean republicanism,
carved soon after the murder of
the nightmarish Duke Alessandro
de' Medici.

Works by Michelangelo's
followers and contemporaries
are ranged in the immediate
vicinity. **Benvenuto Cellini**
and **Giambologna** are the
best of them, and there's more
Giambologna at the top of the
courtyard staircase, where the
first-floor loggia has been turned
into a menagerie for the bronze
animals and birds he made for
the Medici villa at Castello, just
outside Florence.

The doorway to the right opens
into the Salone del Consiglio
Generale, the museum's second
key room, where the presiding
genius is **Donatello**, the
fountainhead of Renaissance
sculpture. In addition to his great
statue of *St George* the room
holds two figures of *David* – the
later one (1430–40) was the first
freestanding nude figure created

since classical times. A decade later the sculptor produced the strange prancing figure known as *Amor-Atys*, which was mistaken for a genuine statue from classical antiquity – the highest compliment the artist could have wished for. Donatello was just as comfortable with portraiture as with Christian or pagan imagery, as his breathtakingly vivid terracotta *Bust of Niccolò da Uzzano* demonstrates; it may be the earliest Renaissance portrait bust. When the occasion demanded, Donatello could also produce a straightforwardly monumental piece like the nearby *Marzocco* (1418–20), Florence's heraldic lion.

Donatello's master, **Ghiberti**, is represented by his relief of *Abraham's Sacrifice*, his entry in the competition to design the Baptistery doors in 1401 (see p.30), easily missed on the right-hand wall; the treatment of the theme submitted by Brunelleschi, effectively the runner-up, is hung alongside. Set around the walls of the room, a sequence of glazed terracotta Madonnas embodies **Luca della Robbia**'s sweet-natured humanism.

The rest of this floor is occupied by a superb collection of European and Islamic applied art, with dazzling specimens of work in enamel, glass, silver, majolica and ivory: among the ivory pieces from Byzantium and medieval France you'll find combs, boxes, chess pieces, and devotional panels featuring scores of figures crammed into a space the size of a paperback.

Sculpture resumes upstairs, with a room largely devoted to the della Robbia family, a prelude to the **Sala dei Bronzetti**, Italy's best assembly of small Renaissance bronzes. Also on this floor there's another roomful of della Robbias and a splendid display of bronze medals, featuring specimens from

the great pioneer of this form of portable art, Pisanello. Lastly, there's a room devoted mainly to **Renaissance portrait busts**, where the centrepiece is Verrocchio's *David*, clearly influenced by the Donatello figure downstairs. Around the walls you'll find Mino da Fiesole's busts of Giovanni de' Medici and Piero il Gottoso (the sons of Cosimo de' Medici), Antonio del Pollaiuolo's *Young Cavalier* (which is probably another Medici portrait), and a bust labelled *Ritratto d'Ignoto* (Portrait of an Unknown Man), which may in fact depict Macchiavelli. Other outstanding pieces include Francesco Laurana's *Battista Sforza*, the *Woman Holding Flowers* by Verrocchio, and the fraught marble relief in which Verrocchio portrays the death of Francesca Tornabuoni-Pitti, from whose tomb this panel was taken.

Mercury by Giambologna

Dante

Dante Alighieri was born in 1265 into a minor noble family. He was educated at Bologna and later at Padua, where he studied philosophy and astronomy. The defining moment in his life came in 1274 when he met the 8-year-old **Beatrice Portinari**. Himself aged just 9 at the time, Dante later described the encounter by quoting the words of Homer: "She appeared to be born not of mortal man but of God." Unhappily, Beatrice's family had decided their daughter was to marry someone else – Simone de' Bardi. The ceremony took

Statue of Dante outside Santa Croce

place when she was 17; seven years later she was dead. Dante, for his part, had been promised – aged 12 – to Gemma Donati. The wedding took place in 1295, when the poet was 30.

In 1289 he fought for Florence against Arezzo and helped in a campaign against Pisa. Eleven years later he was dispatched to San Gimignano, where he was entrusted with the job of coaxing the town into an alliance against Pope Boniface VIII, who had designs on Tuscany. In June of the same year he sought to settle the widening breach between the Black (anti-imperial) and White (more conciliatory) factions of Florence's ruling Guelph party. The Black Guelphs eventually emerged triumphant, and Dante's White sympathies sealed his fate. In 1302, following trumped-up charges of corruption, he was sentenced with other Whites to two years' exile. Rejecting his city of "self-made men and fast-got gain", Dante wandered between Forlì, Verona, Padua, Luni and Venice, writing much of **The Divine Comedy** as he went, before finally settling in Ravenna, where he died in 1321.

Running to more than 14,000 lines, *La Commedia* (the *Divina* was added after Dante's death) is an extraordinarily rich allegory, recounting the poet's journey through *Inferno* (Hell), *Purgatorio* (Purgatory), and *Paradiso* (Paradise), accompanied initially by the Roman poet Virgil and then by Beatrice. Each of these three realms of the dead is depicted in 33 *canti* (a "prologue" to the *Inferno* brings the total up to 100), composed in a verse scheme called *terza rima*, in which lines of eleven syllables follow the rhyme scheme aba, bcb, cdc, ded, etc. Within this framework Dante achieves an amazing variety of tone, encompassing everything from the desperate abuse of the damned to the exalted lyricism of his vision of heaven. Equally remarkable is the fact that Dante wrote his poem in the Tuscan dialect, at a time when Latin was regarded as the only language suitable for serious subjects. Before *La Commedia*, Tuscan was the language of the street; afterwards, it began to be seen as the language of all Italian people, from peasants to philosophers.

The Casa di Dante

MAP p.38, POCKET MAP D11
Via Santa Margherita 1 ⓦ museocasadi
dante.it. April–Sept daily 10am–6pm; Oct–
March Tues–Sun 10am–5pm. €4.

Fraudulently marketed as Dante's
house, the Casa di Dante is
actually a medieval pastiche
dating from 1910. The museum is
a homage to the poet rather than a
shrine: it contains nothing directly
related to his life, and it's likely
Dante was born not on this site
but somewhere in the street that
bears his name. Many editions
of the *Divina Commedia* are on
show, with copies of Botticelli's
illustrations to the poem and a
variety of displays.

Santa Margherita de' Cerchi

MAP p.38, POCKET MAP D11
Via Santa Margherita. Mon–Sat 10am–noon
& 3–5pm, Sun 10am–noon. Free.

Folklore has it that Dante married
his wife, Gemma Donati, in the
eleventh-century church of Santa
Margherita de' Cerchi. There's
no evidence for the claim, but
the building does contain tombs
belonging to the Portinari,
Beatrice's family; the porch also
features the Donati family crest, as
this was their local parish church.
The church is worth a look chiefly
for its altarpiece of the *Madonna
and Four Saints* by Neri di Bicci.

San Martino del Vescovo

MAP p.38, POCKET MAP C12–D12
Piazza San Martino. Mon–Thurs & Sat
10am–noon & 3–5pm, Fri 10am–noon. Free.

The tiny San Martino del Vescovo
stands on the site of an oratory
that served as the Alighieris'
parish church. Rebuilt in 1479, it
later became the headquarters of
the **Compagnia di Buonomini**,
a charitable body dedicated to
aiding impoverished citizens
for whom begging was too
demeaning. The Buonomini
commissioned from Ghirlandaio's
workshop a sequence of frescoes
showing altruistic acts and scenes
from the life of St Martin, and the
result is as absorbing a record of
daily life in Renaissance Florence
as are the Ghirlandaio frescoes in
Santa Maria Novella.

The Torre della Castagna

MAP p.38, POCKET MAP D11–D12
Piazza San Martino.

Opposite San Martino del Vescovo
soars the thirteenth-century Torre
della Castagna, meeting place
of the city's *Priori* before they
decamped to the Palazzo Vecchio.
This is one of the most striking
remnants of Florence's medieval
townscape, when more than 150
such towers rose between the river
and the Duomo, many of them
over two hundred feet high. Allied
clans would link their towers with
wooden catwalks, creating a sort
of upper-class promenade above
the heads of the lowlier citizens. In
1250 the government of the *Primo
Popolo* ordered that the towers
be reduced by two-thirds of their
height; the resulting rubble was
voluminous enough to extend the
city walls beyond the Arno.

San Martino del Vescovo

Orsanmichele

MAP p.38, POCKET MAP C12
Via dei Calzaiuoli. Daily 10am–5pm. Free.

Looming like a fortress over Via dei Calzaiuoli, the foursquare **Orsanmichele** is the oddest church in Florence – a unique hybrid of the sacred and secular, it resembles no other church in the city, and it's not even immediately apparent which of its walls is the front. It's a major monument in itself, and its exterior was once the most impressive outdoor sculpture gallery in the city. Nowadays all of the pieces outside are replicas; most of the originals are in the attached museum.

The first building here was a small oratory secreted in the vegetable garden (*orto*) of a now-vanished Benedictine monastery. A larger church stood on the site from the ninth century: San Michele ad Hortum, later San Michele in Orte –

Orsanmichele

hence the compacted form of Orsanmichele. This church was replaced by a grain market in the thirteenth century, and this in turn was replaced by a loggia designed to serve as a trade hall for the *Arti Maggiori*, the Great Guilds which governed the city. Between 1367 and 1380 the loggia was walled in, after which the site was again dedicated almost exclusively to religious functions, while the two upper storeys were used as emergency grain stores. It was the guilds who paid for the sculptures, which include Ghiberti's *John the Baptist* (the earliest life-size bronze statue of the Renaissance), Verrocchio's *The Incredulity of St Thomas*, Brunelleschi's *St Peter*, and Donatello's *St George* and *St Mark*.

Inside, the centrepiece is a pavilion-sized glass and marble **tabernacle** by Orcagna, the only significant sculptural work by the artist. Decorated with lapis lazuli, stained glass and gold, it frames a Madonna painted in 1347 by Bernardo Daddi as a replacement for the miraculous image of the Virgin, which was destroyed by a fire in 1304. The brotherhood that administered Orsanmichele paid for the tabernacle from thanksgiving donations in the aftermath of the Black Death; so many people attributed their survival to the Madonna's intervention that the money received in 1348 alone was greater than the annual tax income of the city coffers.

Upstairs, the vaulted halls of the granary house the **Museo di Orsanmichele** (Mon 10am–5pm; free), which is entered via the footbridge from the Palazzo dell'Arte della Lana, the building opposite the church entrance. The hall itself is remarkable, and it's home to the original versions of most of the exterior statues.

Shops

Coin

MAP p.38, POCKET MAP C11
Via dei Calzaiuoli 56r ☏ 055 280 531,
🖵 coin.it. Mon–Sat 10am–8pm, Sun
10.30am–8pm.

A clothes-dominated chain
store in an excellent central
position. Quality is generally
high, though styles are fairly
conservative except for one or
two youth-oriented franchises
on the ground floor. Also a
good place for linen and other
household goods, and the
perfume hall has a decent range.

Spezierie Palazzo Vecchio

MAP p.38, POCKET MAP C12
Via Vaccchereccia 9r ☏ 055 239 6055.
Mon–Sat 10am–7.30pm.

This celebrated old shop sells
its own natural remedies and
a range of unique (and not too
expensive) perfumes, such as
Acqua di Caterina de' Medici,
which is based on a sixteenth-
century recipe.

Torrini

MAP p.38, POCKET MAP D12
Via della Condotta 20r ☏ 055 480 157,
🖵 torrinifotogiornalismo.it. Daily
9.30am–7.30pm.

The Torrini archive, founded in
1944 by photojournalist Giulio
Torrini, is a great source of
unusual postcards and prints
of Florence.

Gelateria

Perchè No!

MAP p.38, POCKET MAP C11
Via de' Tavolini 19r. Mon, Wed–Fri &
Sun noon–11pm, Tues noon–8pm, Sat
11am–midnight.

This superb *gelateria* has been in
business since the 1930s; go for
the *crema*, the chocolate or the
gorgeous pistachio.

Cafés, bars & snacks

All'Antico Vinaio

MAP p.38, POCKET MAP D13
Via dei Neri 65r. Daily 10am–3pm &
7–10pm; closed 3 weeks in late July
& early Aug.

Though recently revamped, this
place preserves much of the rough-
and-ready atmosphere that's made it
one of Florence's most popular wine
bars for the past hundred years. The
focacce are famously huge and good,
and the queues perpetual. Simple
meals are served at the tables in the
other branch, over the road at 76r.

Cantinetta dei Verrazzano

MAP p.38, POCKET MAP C11
Via de' Tavolini 18–20r ☏ 055 268 590.
Mon–Sat 8am–9pm, Sun 10am–4.30pm.

Owned by Castello dei Verrazzano,
a major Chianti vineyard, this
wood-panelled place near
Orsanmichele is part-bar, part-café
and part-bakery, making its own
excellent pizza, *focaccia* and cakes.
A perfect spot for a light lunch or
an early evening glass.

Ice cream from Perchè No!

I Fratellini

MAP p.38, POCKET MAP C12
Via dei Cimatori 38r. Daily 10am–7pm.

This minuscule stand-up bar – which attracts a melée most lunchtimes – has been in operation since the 1870s; Armando and Michele, the current proprietors, serve 29 varieties of panini, and local wines by the glass.

Il Cernacchino

MAP p.38, POCKET MAP C12
Via Condotta 38r. Mon–Sat 9.30am–7.30pm.

Substantial and succulent sandwiches, prepared by very friendly people, just a few yards from Piazza della Signoria. There are a few seats at ground level, and more upstairs.

'Ino

MAP p.38, POCKET MAP C13
Via de' Georgofili 3–7r ☏ 055 219 208, ⊕ inofirenze.com. Daily noon–4.30pm.

Part-delicatessen and part-sandwich bar, 'Ino serves what are possibly the most delectable panini in Florence, all made to order, using only the finest ingredients. The wine on offer is similarly fine.

La Prosciutteria

MAP p.38, POCKET MAP D13
Via dei Neri 54r. Daily 10.30am–11pm.

Always packed at lunchtime and in the evening, the *Prosciutteria* is a sort of neo-*vinaio*, serving low-price but perfectly good wine, and big platters of delicious cold meats and cheese to accompany the booze.

Rivoire

MAP p.38, POCKET MAP C12
Piazza della Signoria 5r ☏ 055 221 4412, ⊕ rivoire.it. Tues–Sun 7.30am–9pm.

If you want to people-watch on Florence's main square, this is the place to do so, and the outside tables are invariably packed. Founded in 1872, the café started life specializing in hot chocolate, and chocolate is still its main claim to fame. Ice creams are also good, but the sandwiches and snacks are grotesquely overpriced.

Restaurants

Antico Fattore

MAP p.38, POCKET MAP C13
Via Lambertesca 1–3r ☏ 055 288 975, ⊕ anticofattore.it. Mon–Sat noon–2.45pm & 7–10.30pm; closed Aug.

Rivoire

Simple Tuscan dishes dominate the menu at this classic Florentine trattoria, which has barely changed its look since the 1920s. With main courses well under €20, it's remarkable value.

Gustavino

MAP p.38, POCKET MAP C12
Via della Condotta 37r ☎ 055 239 9806, Ⓦ gustavino.it. Daily noon–11pm.

This smart restaurant-pizzeria – with a kitchen that's in full view, both from the tables and from the street – is perhaps the best place for a full meal in the immediate vicinity of Piazza della Signoria. Tuscan staples, such as bistecca, feature prominently on a menu that has main courses from around €15; a fine selection of wines, too.

Ora d'Aria

MAP p.38, POCKET MAP C13
Via dei Georgofili 11r ☎ 055 200 1699, Ⓦ oradariaristorante.com. Mon 7.30–10pm, Tues–Sat 12.30–3pm & 7.30–10pm; closed two weeks Aug.

Marco Stabile, the young boss of *Ora d'Aria*, has rapidly established a reputation as one of the city's best restaurateurs, thanks to menus that offer a high-quality mix of the traditional and the innovative. The tasting menus (€70) are very good value for such exceptional cooking; and there's an extraordinary 10-part tasting menu for €150 per person (available only if the whole table orders it); à la carte, main courses are in the region of €40. The bright and cool setting is the very opposite of the faux-rustic style that you often find elsewhere in Florence.

Vini e Vecchi Sapori

MAP p.38, POCKET MAP D12
Via dei Magazzini 3r ☎ 055 293 045. Tues–Sat 12.30–2.30pm & 7.30–10pm, Sun 12.30–2.30pm only.

Just off the piazza, this tiny family-run trattoria is always packed – hardly surprising, as it offers four-square traditional Florentine food at prices much lower than its high-toned neighbours.

Yellow Bar

Yellow Bar

MAP p.38, POCKET MAP D11
Via del Proconsolo 39r ☎ 055 211 766. Tues–Sun noon–3pm & 7pm–midnight.

This place looks like a fast-food joint, but the queues of Florentines waiting for a table give you a clue that first impressions are misleading. Inside, the convivial atmosphere in the large dining room is matched by superlative pan-Italian food (including excellent pizzas) in large portions at very reasonable prices. When the main dining room is busy you can often get a table in the mildly less appealing rooms downstairs.

Clubs

Blob Club

MAP p.38, POCKET MAP D13
Via Vinegia 21r ☎ 055 211 209. Oct–April Mon–Wed & Sun 11pm–3am, Thurs–Sat 11pm–5am.

A favourite with Florentine students, possibly on account of its free admission and the 6–9pm happy hour. Seating upstairs, bar and tiny dancefloor downstairs, but don't expect to do much dancing – later on, especially on weekend nights, *Blob* gets packed full with a very happy and very drunken crowd.

West of the centre

Despite the urban improvement schemes of the nineteenth century and the damage inflicted during World War II, several of the streets immediately to the west of Piazza della Signoria retain their medieval character: an amble along Via Porta Rossa, Via delle Terme and Borgo Santi Apostoli will give you some idea of the feel of Florence in the Middle Ages, when every big house was an urban fortress. The best-preserved of these medieval redoubts is the Palazzo Davanzati, whose interior looks little different from the way it did six hundred years ago. The exquisite ancient church of Santi Apostoli is nearby, as is the church of Santa Trìnita, which is home to an outstanding fresco cycle by Domenico Ghirlandaio. Beyond the glitzy Via de' Tornabuoni – the city's priciest slice of retail real estate – you'll find Ognissanti, which also has some outstanding paintings, but the major monument in this area is the fresco-filled church of Santa Maria Novella, which stands opposite the train station.

The Mercato Nuovo

MAP p.56, POCKET MAP B12

Piazza di Mercato Nuovo. Daily: mid–March to Oct 9am–8pm; Nov to mid–March 9am–6.30pm.

The Mercato Nuovo, or Mercato del Porcellino, has been the site of a market since the eleventh century, though the present loggia dates from the sixteenth. Having forked out their euros at the souvenir stalls, most people join the small group that's invariably gathered round the bronze boar known as *Il*

Il Porcellino

Porcellino: you're supposed to earn good luck by getting a coin to fall from the animal's mouth through the grille below his head.

Palazzo Davanzati

MAP p.56, POCKET MAP B12
Via Porta Rossa 13 ⓦ uffizi.firenze.it.
Tues–Sun 8.15am–1.50pm, plus second
& fourth Mon of month. €6. Visitors
have unrestricted access to the first
floor; visits to the second and third
floors are at 10am, 11am & noon, and
must be pre-booked.

Virtually every room of the fourteenth-century Palazzo Davanzati is furnished and decorated in medieval style, using genuine artefacts gathered from a variety of sources.

Merchants' houses in that period would typically have had elaborately **painted walls** in the main rooms, and the Palazzo Davanzati preserves some fine examples of such decor – especially in the dining room. Before the development of systems of credit, wealth had to be sunk into assets such as the tapestries, ceramics, sculpture and lacework that alleviate the austerity of many of these rooms; any surplus cash would have been locked away in a strongbox like the extraordinary example in the **Sala Piccola**. There's also a fine collection of *cassoni*, the painted chests in which the wife's dowry would be stored.

Plushest of the rooms is the first-floor bedroom, but the spot where the occupants would have been likeliest to linger is the **kitchen**. Located on the top floor to minimize the damage that might be caused by the outbreak of a fire, it would have been the warmest room in the house. A load of ancient utensils are on show here, and set into one wall there is the most civilized of amenities, a service shaft connecting the kitchen to all floors of the

Santi Apostoli

building. The leaded glass would have been considered a marvel at a time when many windows were covered with turpentine-soaked rags stretched across frames to repel rainwater.

Santi Apostoli

MAP p.56, POCKET MAP B12–B13
Piazza del Limbo. Tues–Fri 4–7pm. Free.

Legend has it that the church of Santi Apostoli was founded by Charlemagne; it's not quite that ancient, but certainly pre-dates the end of the first millennium. Side chapels were added in the fifteenth and sixteenth centuries, yet the building still has an austere beauty quite unlike any other church in the city centre, with its expanses of bare stone wall and columns of green Prato marble.

The chief treasures of Santi Apostoli are some stone fragments from the Holy Sepulchre in Jerusalem, which on Holy Saturday are used to spark the flame that ignites the "dove" which in turn sets off the fireworks in front of the Duomo.

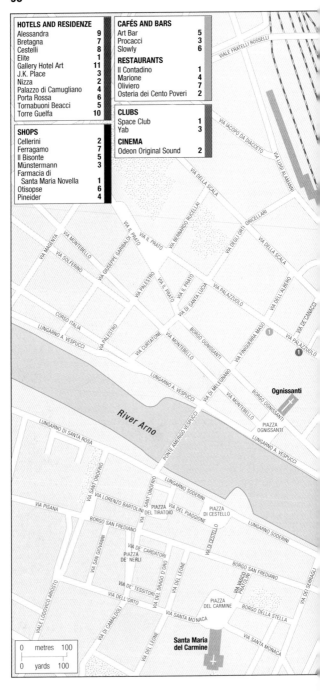

HOTELS AND RESIDENZE

Alessandra	9
Bretagna	7
Cestelli	8
Elite	1
Gallery Hotel Art	11
J.K. Place	3
Nizza	2
Palazzo di Camugliano	4
Porta Rossa	6
Tornabuoni Beacci	5
Torre Guelfa	10

SHOPS

Cellerini	2
Ferragamo	7
Il Bisonte	5
Münstermann	3
Farmacia di Santa Maria Novella	1
Otisopse	6
Pineider	4

CAFÉS AND BARS

Art Bar	5
Procacci	3
Slowly	6

RESTAURANTS

Il Contadino	1
Marione	4
Oliviero	7
Osteria dei Cento Poveri	2

CLUBS

Space Club	1
Yab	3

CINEMA

Odeon Original Sound	2

River Arno

Ognissanti

Santa Maria del Carmine

0	metres	100
0	yards	100

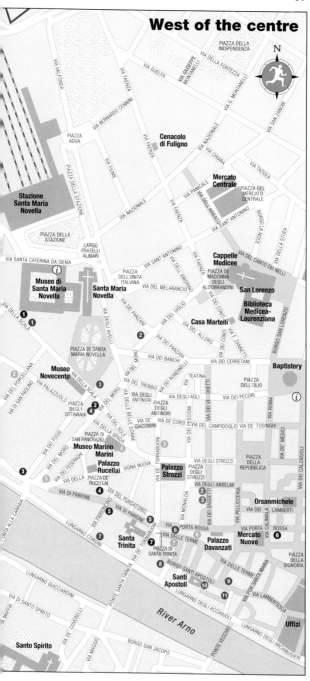

West of the centre

N

PIAZZA DELLA INDIPENDENZA

PIAZZA DELLA FORTEZZA

VIA VALFONDA

VIA GIUSEPPE MONTANELLI

VIA DELLA FORTEZZA

VIA GUELFA

VIA G. MONTANELLI

VIA SAN ZANOBI

VIA FAENZA

VIA BERNARDO CENNINI

PIAZZA ADUA

Cenacolo di Fuligno

VIA FAENZA

VIA NAZIONALE

VIA CHIARA

VIA TADDEA

VIA FIUME

Mercato Centrale

PIAZZA DEL MERCATO CENTRALE

PIAZZA DELLA STAZIONE

Stazione Santa Maria Novella

VIA NAZIONALE

VIA FAENZA

VIA PANICALE

VIA DELL'ARIENTO

VIA SANT'ANTONINO

BORGO LA NOCE

VIA DELLA STUFA

PIAZZA DELLA STAZIONE

LARGO FRATELLI ALINARI

VIA SANTA CATERINA DA SIENA

VIA SANT'ANTONINO

VIA DELL'AMORINO

Cappelle Medicee

VIA DEL CANTO DEI NELLI

ⓘ

❶
❶

Museo di Santa Maria Novella

Santa Maria Novella

PIAZZA DELL'UNITA ITALIANA

VIA DEL MELARANCIO

VIA FAENZA

PIAZZA DI MADONNA DEGLI ALDOBRANDINI

San Lorenzo

Biblioteca Medicea-Laurenziana

VIA DELLA SCALA

VIA DEI PANZANI

VIA DEL GIGLIO

VIA DE' CONTI

BORGO SAN LORENZO

VIA F. ZANETTI

Casa Martelli

VIA DEGLI AVELLI

VIA DEI PANZANI

VIA DEL MORO

VIA DEI BANCHI

VIA DEI CERRETANI

❷

PIAZZA DI SANTA MARIA NOVELLA

Baptistery

❷

VIA DEI PORCELLANA

Museo Novecento

VIA DELLA SCALA

VIA DEL MORO

VIA DEL TREBBIO

VIA DE' RONDINELLI

TEATINA

PIAZZA DELL'OLIO

PIAZZA DEI PECORI

VIA ROMA

ⓘ

VIA SAN PAOLINO

VIA PALAZZUOLO

PIAZZA DEGLI OTTAVIANI

VIA DEGLI ANTINORI

PIAZZA ANTINORI

VIA DEGLI AGLI

VIA DE' VECCHIETTI

❸
❷
❹

VIA DELLE BELLE DONNE

VIA DE' GIACOMINI

VIA DE' CORSI

VIA DEL CAMPIDOGLIO

VIA DE' TOSINGHI

VIA DE' MEDICI

VIA DEI CALZAIUOLI

VIA DELLA SPADA

VIA DEI FOSSI

VIA DEL MORO

VIA DEI FEDERIGHI

PIAZZA DI SAN PANCRAZIO

Museo Marino Marini

VIGNA NUOVA

VIA DE' SASSETTI

VIA DE' TORNABUONI

VIA DEGLI STROZZI

PIAZZA DELLA REPUBBLICA

VIA DELLA VIGNA NUOVA

Palazzo Rucellai

Palazzo Strozzi

PIAZZA DEGLI STROZZI

VIA DEGLI ANSELMI

VIA PELLICCERIA

Orsanmichele

VIA DEI LAMBERTI

❸

PIAZZA DE' RUCELLAI

VIA DEL PURGATORIO

VIA MONALDA

❷
❸

VIA DELLA

❹

VIA DI PARIONE

VIA DI PARIONE

PORTA ROSSA

VIA PORTA ROSSA

CALIMALA

❻

LUNGARNO CORSINI

VIA DELLA SPADA

❺

❺

VIA DELLE TERME

Mercato Nuovo

❼

Santa Trinita

PIAZZA DI SANTA TRINITA

Palazzo Davanzati

VIA POR SANTA MARIA

PIAZZA DELLA SIGNORIA

❼

BORGO SANTI APOSTOLI

VIA DELLE TERME

UNITA ALLA CARRAIA

VIA DEI CONVERELLI

❽

Santi Apostoli

❾

VIA LAMBERTESCA

LUNGARNO GUICCIARDINI

❿
⓫

VIA POR SANTA MARIA

VIA DI SANTO SPIRITO

PONTE SANTA TRINITA

LUNGARNO DEGLI ACCIAIUOLI

Uffizi

VIA MAFFIA

VIA DE' TORNABUONI

LUNGARNO DEGLI ARCHIBUSIERI

River Arno

Santo Spirito

VIA MAGGIO

BORGO SAN JACOPO

PONTE VECCHIO

Santa Trìnita

MAP p.56, POCKET MAP A12
Mon–Sat 8.30am–noon & 4–6pm, Sun 8.30–10.45am & 4–6pm. Free.

Santa Trìnita was founded in 1092 by a Florentine nobleman called **Giovanni Gualberto**, scenes from whose life are illustrated in the frescoes in the fourth chapel of the left aisle. One Good Friday, so the story goes, Gualberto set off intent on avenging the murder of his brother. On finding the murderer he decided to spare his life – it was Good Friday – and proceeded to San Miniato (see p.112), where a crucifix is said to have bowed its head to honour his act of mercy. Giovanni went on to become a Benedictine monk and founded the reforming Vallombrosan order and – notwithstanding the mayhem created on Florence's streets by his militant supporters – was eventually canonized.

The church was rebuilt between about 1300 and 1330, and piecemeal additions over the years have lent it a pleasantly hybrid air: the largely Gothic interior

contrasts with the Mannerist facade, itself at odds with the Romanesque front wall of the interior. The fame of the building is due chiefly to Ghirlandaio's **frescoes** (1483–86) of scenes from the life of St Francis, in the Cappella Sassetti.

Commissioned by Francesco Sassetti, a friend of Lorenzo the Magnificent, these scenes were intended, in part, to eclipse the chapel in Santa Maria Novella sponsored by Sassetti's rival, Giovanni Tornabuoni, which was also painted by Ghirlandaio. St Francis, floating in the sky, is shown bringing a child back to life in Piazza Santa Trìnita, with the church in the background. (Opposite the church you can see the child plummeting to his temporary death.) Above this scene, *St Francis Receiving the Rule* sets the action in Piazza della Signoria and features (right foreground) a portrait of Sassetti between his son, Federigo, and Lorenzo il Magnifico (Sassetti was general manager of the Medici bank). On the steps below them are the humanist Poliziano and

Ponte Santa Trìnita

three of his pupils, Lorenzo's sons;
the blond boy at the back of the
line is Giovanni, the future Pope
Leo X. Ghirlandaio has depicted
himself in the lower scene, with
his hand on his hip, and is also
present in the chapel's altarpiece,
the *Adoration of the Shepherds*
(1485) – he's the shepherd
pointing to the Child and, by
way of self-identification, to the
garland (*ghirlanda*). The figures of
the donors – Sassetti and his wife,
Nera Corsi – kneel to either side;
they are buried in Giuliano da
Sangallo's black tombs under the
side arches.

Displayed in the neighbouring
Cappella Doni is the miraculous
crucifix that bowed its head
to Gualberto. The third of the
church's major works, a powerful
composition by Luca della Robbia
– the tomb of Benozzo Federighi,
bishop of Fiesole – occupies the
left wall of the Cappella Scali, the
farthest chapel.

Ponte Santa Trìnita

MAP p.56, POCKET MAP A12–A13

The sleek Ponte Santa Trìnita was
built on Cosimo I's orders after
its predecessor was demolished
in a flood. The roads on both
banks were raised and widened to
accentuate the dramatic potential
of the new link between the city
centre and the Oltrarno, but what
makes this the classiest bridge in
Florence is the sensuous **curve** of
its arches, a curve so shallow that
engineers have been baffled as to
how the bridge bears up under the
strain. Ostensibly the design was
devised by **Ammannati**, one of the
Medici's favourite artists, but the
curves so closely resemble the arc
of Michelangelo's Medici tombs
that it's likely the credit belongs
to him.

In 1944 the Nazis blew the
bridge to smithereens and
seven years later it was decided
to rebuild it using as much of
the original material as could

Via de' Tornabuoni

be dredged from the Arno. To
ensure maximum authenticity,
all the new stone that was needed
was quarried from the Bóboli
gardens, where the stone for
Ammannati's bridge had been
cut. Twelve years after the war
ended, the reconstructed bridge
was completed.

Via de' Tornabuoni

MAP p.56, POCKET MAP A12

The shops of Via de' Tornabuoni
are effectively out of bounds
to those who don't travel first
class. Versace, Ferragamo, Prada,
Cavalli, Gucci and Armani have
their outlets here: indeed, in
recent years they have come
to monopolize the street (and
some of its tributaries), to the
dismay of many, who see further
evidence of the loss of Florentine
identity in the eviction of local
institutions such as the Seeber
bookshop, the Farmacia Inglese
and the *Giacosa* café – the last of
these lives on in name only, as
the café of Palazzo Strozzi and as
an adjunct to the huge Roberto
Cavalli shop.

Palazzo Strozzi

MAP p.56, POCKET MAP A11
Piazza degli Strozzi Ⓦ palazzostrozzi.org.

Conspicuous wealth is nothing
new on Via de' Tornabuoni.
Looming above everything is the
vast Palazzo Strozzi, the largest
and most intimidating of all
Florentine Renaissance palaces,
with windows as big as gateways
and embossed with lumps of stone
the size of boulders. Designed
by Giuliano da Sangallo, it was
begun by the banker Filippo
Strozzi, a figure so powerful that
he was once described as "the
first man of Italy", and whose
family were ringleaders of the
anti-Medici faction in Florence.
He bought and demolished a
dozen town houses to make space
for this strongbox in stone, and
its construction lasted from 1489
to 1536. Not until the 1930s did
the Strozzi family relinquish
ownership of the building,
which is now administered by
the Fondazione Palazzo Strozzi,
under whose administration the
building has become a venue for
outstanding art exhibitions; it has
a nice café too.

Palazzo Rucellai

MAP p.56, POCKET MAP C5
Via della Vigna Nuova 18.

In the 1440s Giovanni Rucellai,
one of the richest businessmen in
the city (and an esteemed scholar
too), decided to commission a new
house from **Leon Battista Alberti**,
whose accomplishments as
architect, mathematician, linguist
and theorist of the arts prompted a
contemporary to exclaim, "Where
shall I put Battista Alberti: in
what category of learned men
shall I place him?" The resultant
Palazzo Rucellai, two minutes'
walk from the Strozzi house at
Via della Vigna Nuova 18, was the
first palace in Florence to follow
the rules of classical architecture;
its tiers of pilasters, incised into
smooth blocks of stone, evoke the
exterior wall of the Colosseum.
Alberti later produced another,
equally elegant design for the same
patron – the front of the church of
Santa Maria Novella. In contrast to
the feud between the Medici and
the Strozzi, the Rucellai were on
the closest terms with the city's *de
facto* royal family: the **Loggia dei
Rucellai**, across the street (now a

Palazzo Rucellai

Santa Maria Novella train station

shop), was in all likelihood built for the wedding of Giovanni's son to the granddaughter of Cosimo il Vecchio, and the frieze on the Palazzo Rucellai features the heraldic devices of the two families, the Medici emblem alongside the Rucellai sail.

The Museo Marino Marini and Cappella Rucellai

MAP p.56, POCKET MAP A11
Piazza San Pancrazio Ⓦ **museomarino marini.it. Sat–Mon 10am–7pm, Wed–Fri 10am–1pm. €6.**
Round the corner from the Palazzo Rucellai stands the ex-church of San Pancrazio, deconsecrated by Napoleon, then successively the offices of the state lottery, the magistrates' court, a tobacco factory and an arsenal. It's now the **Museo Marino Marini**, a superbly designed space which holds some two hundred works that were left to the city in Marini's will. Born in Pistoia in 1901, Marini trained at the Accademia and devoted most of his subsequent career to sculpture, developing a distinctive style in which the mythical and the modern were powerfully fused. His equestrian figures are his best-known works, and variations of the theme make a strong showing here, alongside some potent nudes.

Once part of San Pancrazio church and now entered via the Marini museum, the **Cappella Rucellai**, which was redesigned by Alberti, houses the marble-clad **Tempietto dello Santo Sepolcro**, the most exquisite of his architectural creations. Its form is derived from ancient Christian chapels that were themselves built in imitation of the Holy Sepulchre in Jerusalem, and its decoration is derived from Romanesque Tuscan churches such as San Miniato (see p.112). Commissioned by Giovanni Rucellai as his own funerary monument, the Tempietto was completed in 1467, more than a decade before Giovanni's death.

Stazione Santa Maria Novella

MAP p.56, POCKET MAP C3–C4
Most visitors barely spare a glance for Santa Maria Novella train station, but it's a superb building. It was in 1933 that its principal architect, Giovanni Michelucci (1891–1990), won the competition to design a new main rail terminal for the city, and its planning is so impeccably rational that it proved to be adequate for the city's needs until the start of this century.

Santa Maria Novella

MAP p.56, POCKET MAP C4
Piazza Santa Maria Novella. April–Sept
Mon–Thurs 9am–7pm, Fri 11am–7pm,
Sat 9am–5.30pm, Sun 1–5.30pm; Oct–
March Mon–Thurs 9am–5.30pm, Fri
11am–5.30pm, Sat 9am–5pm, Sun
1–5.30pm. €5, with Museo di Santa
Maria Novella.

The graceful church of Santa
Maria Novella was the Florentine
base of the Dominican order, the
vigilantes of thirteenth-century
Catholicism. A more humble
church, Santa Maria delle Vigne,
which had existed here since the
eleventh century, was handed
to the Dominicans in 1221;
they then set about altering the
place to their taste. By 1360 the
interior was finished, but only the
Romanesque lower part of the
facade had been completed. This
state of affairs lasted until 1456,
when Giovanni Rucellai paid for
Alberti to design a classical upper
storey that would blend with the
older section while improving

Santa Maria Novella

the facade's proportions. The
sponsor's name is picked out
across the facade in Roman
capitals, while the Rucellai family
emblem, the billowing sail of
Fortune, runs as a motif through
the central frieze.

Santa Maria Novella's **interior**,
which was designed to enable
preachers to address their
sermons to as large a congregation
as possible, is adorned with a
ground-breaking painting by
Masaccio, a crucifix by Giotto and
no fewer than three major fresco
cycles. **Masaccio**'s extraordinary
1427 depiction of the **Trinity**,
painted on the wall of the left
aisle, was one of the earliest works
in which the rules of perspective
and classical proportion were
rigorously employed, and
Florentines queued to view the
illusion on its unveiling, stunned
by a painting which appeared to
create three-dimensional space on
a solid wall.

Giotto's crucifix, a radically
naturalistic and probably very
early work (c.1288–90), hangs in
what is thought to be its intended
position, poised dramatically over
the centre of the nave. Hitherto,
it had been hidden away in the
sacristy, veiled by a layer of dirt so
thick that many scholars refused
to recognize it as the work of the
master; the attribution is still
disputed by some.

The chapel to the right of the
chancel is covered with a fabulous
cycle of frescoes commissioned in
1489 from **Filippino Lippi** by the
banker Filippo Strozzi. Illustrating
the life of Strozzi's namesake,
St Philip the Apostle, the paintings
were commenced after Filippino
had spent some time in Rome,
and the work he carried out on his
return displays an archeologist's
obsession with ancient Roman
culture. Behind the altar is
Strozzi's tomb (1491–95),
beautifully carved by Benedetto
da Maiano.

The interior of Santa Maria Novella

As a chronicle of fifteenth-century life in Florence, no series of frescoes is more fascinating than **Domenico Ghirlandaio**'s pictures around the chancel and high altar. The artist's masterpiece, the pictures were commissioned by Giovanni Tornabuoni, a banker and uncle of Lorenzo de' Medici (Lorenzo the Magnificent), which explains why certain illustrious ladies of the Tornabuoni family are present at the births of both John the Baptist and the Virgin. These frescoes are a proud celebration of Florence at its zenith – indeed, one of the frescoes includes a Latin inscription which reads: "The year 1490, when the most beautiful city renowned for abundance, victories, arts and noble buildings profoundly enjoyed salubrity and peace." Ghirlandaio himself features in the scene in which Joachim, the Virgin's father, is chased from the temple because he has been unable to have children – the painter is the figure in the right-hand group with hand on hip.

The church's third great fresco cycle is in the **Cappella Strozzi**, which lies above the level of the rest of the church at the end of the left transept. Commissioned in 1350 as an expiation of the sin of usury by Tommaso Strozzi, an ancestor of Filippo Strozzi, the pictures are the masterpiece of Nardo di Cione, brother of the better-known Orcagna (Andrea di Cione), who painted the chapel's magnificent high altarpiece, *Christ Presenting the Keys to St Peter and the Book of Wisdom to Thomas Aquinas* (1357). Behind the altar, the central fresco depicts the *Last Judgement*, with Dante featured as one of the saved (in white, third from the left, second row from the top). So, too, are Tommaso Strozzi and his wife, shown being led by St Michael into paradise, with an angel helping the righteous up through a trapdoor; on the right of the altar, a devil forks the damned down into hell. The theme of judgement is continued in the fresco of Dante's *Inferno* on the right wall, faced by a thronged *Paradiso*.

The adjacent chapel, the Cappella Gondi, contains a crucifix carved by Brunelleschi, supposedly as a riposte to the uncouthness of Donatello's crucifix in Santa Croce.

The Museo di Santa Maria Novella

MAP p.56, POCKET MAP C4
Piazza Santa Maria Novella, entered via the church or at Piazza della Stazione 4 ⓦ museicivicifiorentini.comune.fi.it. April–Sept Mon–Thurs 9am–7pm, Fri 11am–7pm, Sat 9am–5.30pm, Sun 1–5.30pm; Oct–March Mon–Thurs 9am–5.30pm, Fri 11am–5.30pm, Sat 9am–5pm, Sun 1–5.30pm. €5, with church of Santa Maria Novella.

Remarkable paintings are housed in the spacious Romanesque conventual buildings of Santa Maria Novella, now home to the Museo di Santa Maria Novella. The main cloister, the **Chiostro Verde**, dates from the fourteenth century and features frescoes of *Stories from Genesis* (1425–30) executed by Paolo Uccello and his workshop. The cloister takes its name from the green base *terra verde* pigment they used, and which now gives the paintings a spectral undertone. Best preserved of the frescoes is *The Flood*, a windswept scene rendered almost unintelligible by the telescoping perspective and the double appearance of the Ark (before and after the flood), whose flanks form a receding corridor in the centre of the picture.

Off the cloister opens the **Cappellone degli Spagnoli**, or Spanish Chapel, which received its present name after Eleonora di Toledo, wife of Cosimo I, reserved it for the use of her Spanish entourage. Presumably she derived much inspiration from its majestic fresco cycle (1367–69) by Andrea di Firenze, an extended depiction of the triumph of the Catholic Church that was described by Ruskin as "the most noble piece of pictorial philosophy in Italy". Virtually every patch of the walls is covered with frescoes, whose theme is the role of the Dominicans in the battle against heresy and in the salvation of Christian souls. Most spectacular is the right wall, depicting *The Triumph of the Church*. The Dominicans are of course prominent among the ranks of figures representing religious orders: note St Dominic, the order's

The Paterenes and St Peter Martyr

In the twelfth century, Florence became the crucible of one of the reforming **religious movements** that periodically cropped up in medieval Europe. The Paterenes were convinced that everything worldly was touched by the Devil. Accordingly they despised the papacy for its claims to temporal power, and their campaign against the financial and moral corruption of the Catholic Church inevitably brought them into conflict with Rome. The displeasure of the Vatican found its means of expression in the Dominican known as St Peter Martyr. Operating from Santa Maria Novella, this papal inquisitor headed a couple of anti-Paterene fraternities, which were in effect his private army. In 1244 he led them into battle across Piazza Santa Maria Novella, where they massacred hundreds of the theological enemy. The carnage is commemorated by the Croce al Trebbio in Via delle Belle Donne, off the eastern side of the piazza.

After this, the Dominicans turned to less militant work, founding the charitable organization called the **Misericordia**, which is still in existence today. In 1252 Peter was knifed to death, supposedly by a pair of Paterene heretics; legend relates that the dying man managed to write out the Credo with his own blood before expiring – an incident depicted in the frescoes in Santa Maria Novella's Cappellone degli Spagnoli. Within a year he'd been made a saint.

The triumph of the church in the Cappellone degli Spagnoli

founder, unleashing the "hounds of the lord", or *Domini Canes*, a pun on the Dominicans' name.

The decoration of the Chiostrino dei Morti, the oldest part of the complex, has not aged so robustly, but the Chiostro Grande, the largest cloister in Florence, has extensive sixteenth- and seventeenth-century frescoes of scenes from the life of Christ and St Dominic, while traces of fourteenth-century decoration can be seen in the old dormitory. On the upper floor, the chapel has a gorgeous fresco of St Veronica, painted by the young Pontormo in 1515.

Museo Novecento

MAP p.56, POCKET MAP C5
Piazza Santa Maria Novella 14ar
ⓦ museonovecento.it. April–Sept Mon–Wed
& Sat–Sun 11am–8pm, Thurs 11am–2pm, Fri
11am–11pm; Oct–March Mon–Wed & Fri–Sun
11am–7pm, Thurs 11am–2pm. €8.50.
The colonnaded building facing Santa Maria Novella across the piazza was formerly a hospital, which was founded back in the thirteenth century and rebuilt in the second half of the fifteenth, probably to a design by Michelozzo. Soon after its completion, Andrea della Robbia added the attractive terracotta

medallions to the loggia. In the 1780s it became a crafts school for poor unmarried women, a function it retained until the twentieth century, when it was converted into a school for children. Now, having been restored, it's home to Florence's newest civic museum, the **Museo Novecento**, featuring some of the heavyweights of Italian twentieth-century art, such as Giorgio Morandi, Giorgio de Chirico, Lucio Fontana and Emilio Vedova.

Chiostro Verde, Museo di Santa Maria Novella

Giotto's crucifix in Ognissanti

Ognissanti

MAP p.56, POCKET MAP B5
Borgo Ognissanti. Mon–Sat 9.30am–noon &
4–7pm, Sun 4–7pm. Free.

In medieval times one of
the main areas of cloth
production – the mainstay of
the Florentine economy – was
in the west of the city. San
Salvatore in Ognissanti, the main
church of this quarter, stands
on a piazza that might be taken
as a symbol of the state of the
present-day Florentine economy,
dominated as it is by two of
Florence's plushest hotels. The
church was founded in 1256 by
the Umiliati, a Benedictine order
from Lombardy who specialized
in weaving woollen cloth; in
1561 the Franciscans took over
the church, the new tenure
being marked by a Baroque

overhaul which spared only the
medieval campanile.

The young face squeezed
between the Madonna and
the dark-cloaked man in
Ghirlandaio's *Madonna della
Misericordia* (1473), over the
second altar on the right, is said
to be that of Amerigo Vespucci
(1451–1512), an agent for the
Medici in Seville, whose two
voyages in 1499 and 1501 would
lend his name to a continent.
The altar was paid for by the
Vespucci, a family of silk
merchants from the Ognissanti
district, which is why other
members of the clan appear
beneath the Madonna's cloak.
Among them is Simonetta
Vespucci (at the Virgin's left
hand), the mistress of Giuliano
de' Medici – she is said to have
been the model for the face
of Botticelli's Venus. The idea
may not be so far-fetched,
for Botticelli was born in the
Ognissanti parish and lived
locally, and the Vespucci and
Filipepi families were on good
terms. Botticelli is buried in the
church, beneath a round tomb
slab in the south transept (the
slab bears his baptismal name,
Sandro Filipepi), and his small
fresco of *St Augustine's Vision
of St Jerome* (1480) hangs on
the same wall as the Madonna,
between the third and fourth
altars. Facing it is Ghirlandaio's
more earthbound *St Jerome*, also
painted in 1480; in the same year
Ghirlandaio painted the *Last
Supper* that covers one wall of
the refectory, reached through
the cloister entered to the left
of the church (Mon & Sat 9am–
noon; free). And don't miss the
dazzling **Crucifix** that hangs in
the left transept of Ognissanti: in
2010 it emerged from a seven-
year restoration, and during
cleaning it was established by
infrared and X-ray analysis that
it's almost certainly by Giotto.

Shops

Cellerini

MAP p.56, POCKET MAP C5
Via del Sole 9 ⓣ 055 282 533, ⓦ cellerini
.it. Summer Mon–Fri 11am–1pm & 3–7pm,
Sat 11am–1pm; winter Mon 3–7pm, Tues–
Sat 11am–1pm & 3–7pm.

Bags, bags and more bags, from
the city's premier exponents of the
craft. Their handiwork is elegant,
durable and costly.

Ferragamo

MAP p.56, POCKET MAP A12
Via de' Tornabuoni 14r ⓣ 055 292 123,
ⓦ salvatoreferragamo.it. Daily
10am–7.30pm.

Established by Salvatore
Ferragamo, once the most
famous shoemaker in the world,
Ferragamo now produces ready-
to-wear clothing too, but the
company's reputation still rests
on its beautiful shoes. The shop
is unbelievably grandiose, and
has a museum in the basement,
featuring shoes that Salvatore
made for Marilyn Monroe.

Il Bisonte

MAP p.56, POCKET MAP A12
Via del Parione 31–33r ⓣ 055 215 722,
ⓦ ilbisonte.com. Mon–Sat 9.30am–7pm,
Sun 11.30am–6pm.

Beautiful and robust bags,
briefcases and accessories,
many of them made from
vacchetta, a soft cow-hide that
ages very nicely.

Münstermann

MAP p.56, POCKET MAP C5
Piazza Goldoni 2r ⓣ 055 210 660,
ⓦ munstermann.it. Tues–Sat 10am–1pm
& 2–7pm.

Münstermann has been producing
its own soaps and perfumes since
the end of the nineteenth century,
and the recipes it uses today are
virtually unchanged. So if you
want something a little different
from the usual duty-free offerings,
this is the place.

Farmacia di Santa Maria Novella

MAP p.56, POCKET MAP C4
Via della Scala 16 ⓣ 055 216 276,
ⓦ smnovella.it. Daily 9am–8pm.

Occupying the pharmacy of the
Santa Maria Novella monastery,
this sixteenth-century shop
was founded by Dominican
monks as an outlet for their
potions, ointments and herbal
remedies. Many of these are still
available, including distillations of
flowers, together with face-creams
and shampoos.

Otisopse

MAP p.56, POCKET MAP C12
Via Porta Rossa 13r ⓣ 055 239 6717,
ⓦ otisopse.it. Mon–Sat 9.30am–7pm.

Florentine footwear is of famously
high quality, but can be rather
staid. Otisopse, founded in Naples
in 1929, goes instead for the
cheap and cheerful approach – a
pair of their pink desert boots or
purple moccasins will cost you
around €50. There are three other
branches, all in Oltrarno: Via
Guiccardini 2r and Piazza Nazario
Sauro 7r and 17r.

Farmacia di Santa Maria Novella

Pineider

MAP p.56, POCKET MAP C5
Piazza de' Rucellai 4–7r ☎ 055 284 656,
🅦 pineider.com. Mon–Sat 10am–7pm.

Pineider sells briefcases, picture frames and other accessories for home and office, but its reputation rests on its colour-coordinated calling cards, handmade papers and envelopes – as used by Napoleon, Stendhal, Byron and Shelley, to name just a few past customers.

Cafés & bars

Art Bar

MAP p.56, POCKET MAP C5
Via del Moro 4r ☎ 055 287 661. Daily
7pm–1am.

A fine little bar near Piazza di Carlo Goldoni. The interior looks like an antique shop, while the club-like atmosphere attracts a smart crowd. Busiest at happy hour (6.30–9pm), when the imaginative cocktails are in heavy demand.

Procacci

MAP p.56, POCKET MAP A11
Via de' Tornabuoni 64r ☎ 055 211 656.
Mon–Sat 11am–9pm, Sun 11am–8pm;
closed Aug.

This famous café doesn't serve coffee, just wine and cold drinks.

Slowly

Its reputation comes from the extraordinary, tiny and delicious *tartufati* (truffle-butter brioche).

Slowly

MAP p.56, POCKET MAP B12
Via Porta Rossa 63r ☎ 055 264 5354,
🅦 slowlycafe.com. Mon–Sat noon–2am.

With its black banquettes and ice-blue lighting, *Slowly* is one of the coolest-looking bars in town, and for years it's been one of the main watering holes for Florence's style-conscious and well-heeled young professionals. There's a DJ every night from around 10pm.

Restaurants

Il Contadino

MAP p.56, POCKET MAP B4
Via Palazzuolo 71r ☎ 055 238 2673,
🅦 trattoriailcontadino.com. Daily
noon–10.30pm.

This no-frills trattoria has been popular since it opened for business in the 1970s, and it hasn't changed its style much since then, with its monochrome tiled dining room and refectory-like seating. Service is fast and friendly, and the food is decent and very cheap – a three-course lunch and dinner fixed menu costs as little as €13. No reservations.

Slowly

Art Bar

Marione

MAP p.56, POCKET MAP A11
Via della Spada 27r ☏ 055 214 756. Daily noon–3pm & 7–11pm; closed first two weeks of Aug.

This simple old trattoria is a reliable stand-by. It's not the most refined cooking in Florence, and the ambience is brisk rather than homely, but with main courses all under €15 you can't really complain.

Oliviero

MAP p.56, POCKET MAP A12
Via delle Terme 52r ☏ 055 212 421, Ⓦ ristorante-oliviero.it. Mon–Sat 7–10.30pm; closed Aug.

Soon after opening in 1962, *Oliviero* established itself as one of the city's finest and most glamorous restaurants. It closed in 2016 but reopened later that year with a new chef, Ivan Ferrara, in charge of the kitchen, and a similarly youthful team running the dining room. A graduate of the *Enoteca Pinchiorri*, Ferrara has refreshed the menu, while continuing its tradition of mixing Tuscan classics with fish dishes – something of a rarity in Florence. The full *menu degustazione* is €85 without wine, or €135 with a different wine for each course; there's a more modest version at €65/105. À la carte, main courses are around €30–35.

Osteria dei Cento Poveri

MAP p.56, POCKET MAP C5
Via Palazzuolo 31r & 41r ☏ 055 218 846, Ⓦ centopoveri.it. Daily noon–3pm & 7pm–midnight.

This very popular *osteria* offers more fish than is customary with meat-oriented Tuscan menus, and has some excellent set menus (both fish and meat) starting at €30. Established in the 1990s, the operation has expanded in recent years, and pizzas are served at the newer branch, at 41r.

Clubs

Space Club

MAP p.56, POCKET MAP B4
Via Palazzuolo 37 ☏ 055 293 082. Daily 10pm–4am.

Having operated for years under the name *Space Electronic*, the refurbished *Space Club* is still the archetypal big Continental disco, with Florence's biggest dancefloor.

Yab

MAP p.56, POCKET MAP B12
Via de' Sassetti 5r ☏ 055 215 160, Ⓦ yab. it. Mon & Wed–Sat 8pm–4am; closed June–Sept.

This basement club-bar-restaurant has been popular for years and is known throughout the country for Monday's "Yabsmoove" – Italy's longest-running hip-hop night. The most relaxed and reliable night's clubbing in central Florence.

Cinema

Odeon Original Sound

MAP p.56, POCKET MAP B11
Piazza Strozzi 2 ☏ 055 214 068, Ⓦ odeon firenze.com. Closed for part of Aug.

Mainstream films are screened in their original language (with Italian subtitles) at this air-conditioned cinema almost every day.

North of the centre

The San Lorenzo district, to the northwest of the Duomo, is the city's main market area, with scores of clothing and accessories stalls encircling a vast food hall. Racks of T-shirts, leather jackets and belts fill the road beside the church of San Lorenzo, a building of major importance, to which is attached another of the city's major draws, the Cappelle Medicee (Medici Chapels). While some of the most prominent members of the Medici family are buried in the main part of San Lorenzo, dozens of lesser lights are interred in these chapels, with two of them being celebrated by some of Michelangelo's finest sculptures. The Medici also account for the area's other major sight, the Palazzo Medici-Riccardi, to the north of which lies the Museo di San Marco, replete with paintings by Fra' Angelico. A brief walk from San Marco brings you to the Accademia, famous above all for Michelangelo's David. A short distance to the east is the graceful Piazza Santissima Annunziata, site of Brunelleschi's Spedale degli Innocenti, the superb church of Santissima Annunziata and the Museo Archeologico.

Sagrestia Vecchia, San Lorenzo

San Lorenzo

MAP p.72, POCKET MAP D4
Piazza San Lorenzo Ⓦ operamedicea laurenziana.org. Mon–Sat 10am–5.30pm; March–Oct also Sun 1.30–5.30pm. €6, or €8.50 with Biblioteca Laurenziana.

Founded in 393, San Lorenzo has a claim to be the oldest church in Florence, and for some three hundred years it was the city's cathedral. By 1060 a sizeable Romanesque church had been built on the site, a building which in time became the Medici's parish church. In 1419 Giovanni di Bicci de' Medici, founder of the Medici fortune, offered to finance a new church, designed by **Brunelleschi**, but construction was hampered by financial problems. Giovanni's son, Cosimo de' Medici, eventually saved the day, but his largesse was not sufficient to provide the church with a facade, a feature it still lacks.

San Lorenzo

What strikes you on stepping **inside the church** is the cool rationality of Brunelleschi's design, an instantly calming contrast to the hubbub outside. The first work of art to catch your attention, in the second chapel on the right, is Rosso Fiorentino's *Marriage of the Virgin* (1523), with its golden-haired and youthful Joseph. There's another arresting painting at the top of the left aisle – Bronzino's enormous fresco of *The Martyrdom of St Lawrence* (1569) – but it seems a shallow piece of work alongside the nearby bronze pulpits by Donatello. Clad with reliefs depicting scenes preceding and following the Crucifixion, these are the artist's last works (begun c.1460) and were completed by his pupils as increasing paralysis limited their master's ability to model in wax. Jagged and discomforting, charged with more energy than the space can contain, these panels are more like virtuoso sketches in bronze than conventional reliefs. Donatello is buried in the nave of the church, next to his patron, Cosimo de' Medici, and commemorated by a memorial in the chapel in the north transept, close to Filippo Lippi's altarpiece of the *Annunciation*. Cosimo's own tomb, in the centre of the church, bears the inscription "Pater Patriae" (Father of the Fatherland) – a title once borne by Roman emperors.

Four other eminent Medici lie buried in the **Sagrestia Vecchia**, one of Brunelleschi's earliest projects (1421–26), and the only one completed in his lifetime. The space was commissioned by Giovanni Bicci de' Medici as a private chapel; on his death, Giovanni was buried beneath the massive marble slab at the centre of the chapel, with his wife, Piccarda. Another tomb, on the left as you enter, is the resting place of Giovanni's grandsons, Giovanni and Piero de' Medici. Donatello created the cherub-filled frieze and the eight tondi above it, depicting the Four Evangelists and a quartet of scenes from the life of St John; he was also responsible for the two bronze doors, showing pairs of disputatious martyrs (the left door), and the Apostles and Fathers of the Church (the right).

CAFÉS AND BARS
Casa del Vino 5
La Ménagère 7
Robiglio 6
Zanobini 3

GELATERIA
Carabé 4

RESTAURANTS
Da Mario 1
Sergio Gozzi 8
Zà-Zà 2

HOTELS AND RESIDENZE
Antica Dimora Firenze 5
Antica Dimora Johlea 2
Azzi 14
Casci 15
Kursaal Ausonia 10
Locanda dei Poeti 8
Loggiato dei Serviti 12
Merlini 11
Morandi alla Crocetta 13
Mr. My Resort 4
Orto de' Medici 6
Relais Grand Tour 7
Residenza Castiglioni 16
Residenza Johanna I 1

HOSTELS
Archi Rossi 9
Wow Florence Hostel 3

North of the centre

SHOPS AND MARKETS	
Alinari	2
Mercato Centrale	1
San Lorenzo market	3

The Biblioteca Medicea-Laurenziana

MAP p.72, POCKET MAP D4

Piazza San Lorenzo Ⓦ operamedicea
laurenziana.org. Mon–Fri 9.30am–1.30pm.
€3, or €8.50 with San Lorenzo.

A gateway to the left of San Lorenzo
leads to the Biblioteca Medicea-
Laurenziana. Wishing to create a
suitably grandiose home for the
family's precious manuscripts, Pope
Clement VII – Lorenzo's nephew
– asked Michelangelo to design a
new library in 1524. The **Ricetto**,
or vestibule, of the building he
eventually came up with (more than
thirty years later) is a showpiece of
Mannerist architecture, delighting
in paradoxical display: brackets that
support nothing, columns that sink
into the walls, and a flight of steps so
large that it almost fills the room.

In the reading room, too,
almost everything is the work of
Michelangelo. Exhibitions in the
connecting rooms draw on the
15,000-piece Medici collection,
which includes manuscripts
as diverse as a fifth-century
copy of Virgil – the collection's
oldest item – and a treatise on
architecture by Leonardo.

The Cappelle Medicee

MAP p.72, POCKET MAP D4

Piazza Madonna degli Aldobrandini
Ⓦ bargellomusei.beniculturali.it.
Summer Tues–Sat 8.15am–5pm; winter
8.15am–1.50pm plus 1st, 3rd & 5th Sun of
month and 2nd & 4th Mon of the month,
same hours. €8.

Michelangelo's most celebrated
contribution to the San Lorenzo
complex forms part of the

Michelangelo

Michelangelo Buonarroti (1475–1564) was born in Caprese in
eastern Tuscany, but his family soon moved to Florence, where
he became a pupil of Ghirlandaio, making his first stone reliefs for
Lorenzo de' Medici. After the Medici were expelled from the city
the young Michelangelo went to Rome in 1496. There he secured a
reputation as the **most skilled sculptor** of his day with the *Bacchus*
(now in the Bargello) and the *Pietà* for St Peter's.

After his return to Florence in 1501, Michelangelo carved the
David and the *St Matthew* (both in the Accademia). He was also
employed to paint a fresco of the *Battle of Cascina* in the Palazzo
Vecchio. Only the cartoon was finished, but this became the
single most influential work of art in the city, its twisting nudes
a recurrent motif in later Mannerist art. Work was suspended
in 1505 when Michelangelo was called to Rome by Pope Julius
II to create his tomb; the *Slaves* in the Accademia was intended
for this grandiose project which, like many of Michelangelo's
schemes, was never finished.

In 1508 Michelangelo began his other superhuman project,
the decoration of the **Sistine Chapel** ceiling in Rome. Back in
Florence, he started work on the San Lorenzo complex in 1516,
staying on to supervise its defences when it was besieged by the
Medici and Charles V in 1530. Four years later he left Florence
for good, and spent his last thirty years in Rome, during which he
produced the *Last Judgement* in the Sistine Chapel. Florence has
one work from this final phase of Michelangelo's career, the *Pietà*
he intended for his own tomb (now in the Museo dell'Opera del
Duomo; see p.32).

Cappelle Medicee, which are entered from Piazza Madonna degli Aldobrandini, at the back of the church.

After passing through the crypt, where almost fifty lesser Medici are buried, you climb up to the Cappella dei Principi (Chapel of the Princes), an oppressively colourful stone-plated hall built as a mausoleum for Cosimo I and the grand dukes who succeeded him. Pass straight through for the **Sagrestia Nuova**, which was designed by Michelangelo as a tribute to Brunelleschi's Sagrestia Vecchia in the main body of San Lorenzo. The architecture plays complex games with the visual vocabulary of classical architecture, and provides a magnificent setting for the three **Medici tombs** (1520–34), two of which are wholly by Michelangelo and the other one partly.

The tomb on the left as you enter belongs to Lorenzo, Duke of Urbino, grandson of Lorenzo the Magnificent. Michelangelo depicts him as a man of thought, and his sarcophagus bears figures of *Dawn* and *Dusk*, the times of day whose ambiguities appeal to the contemplative mind. Opposite stands the tomb of Lorenzo de' Medici's youngest son, Giuliano, Duke of Nemours; as a man of action, his character is symbolized by the clear antithesis of *Day* and *Night*.

The two principal effigies were intended to face the equally grand tombs of Lorenzo de' Medici and his brother Giuliano. The only part of the project completed by Michelangelo is the *Madonna and Child*, the last image of the Madonna he ever sculpted. The figures to either side are Cosmas and Damian, patron saints of doctors (*medici*) and the Medici. Although completed by others, they follow Michelangelo's design.

Sagrestia Nuova, Cappelle Medicee

Casa Martelli

MAP p.72, POCKET MAP D4
Via Zannetti 8 📞 055 290 383. Thurs 2–6pm, Sat & first, third & fifth Sun of month 9am–1pm; guided tour hourly (usually in Italian), up to 1hr before closing. €3.

From the sixteenth century until the death of the last of the Martelli in 1989, Casa Martelli was home to a family that for many years was very closely associated with their near neighbours, the Medici. It was not until 1738 that Casa Martelli took on its present form, when several houses were merged to create this spectacular palazzo. The interior was then completely redecorated, and it's the style of this refurbishment that dominates, with room after room of trompe l'oeil frescoes, sumptuous furniture, delicate stucco work and shimmering brocades. The family's art collection, stacked almost to the ceiling in the picture gallery, includes work by Piero di Cosimo, Salvator Rosa and Luca Giordano.

The Palazzo Medici-Riccardi

MAP p.72, POCKET MAP E4
Via Cavour 1 ⓦ **palazzo-medici.it. Mon,**
Tues & Thurs–Sun 8.30am–7pm. €7, or €10
for special exhibitions.

The Palazzo Medici-Riccardi was built for Cosimo de' Medici by Michelozzo between 1444 and 1462, and remained the family headquarters until Cosimo I moved to the Palazzo Vecchio (see p.40) in 1540. In Cosimo de Medici's prime, around fifty members of the clan lived here; Donatello's *Judith and Holofernes* (now in the Palazzo Vecchio) adorned the walled garden, while the same artist's *David* (now in the Bargello) stood in the entrance courtyard.

The palace now houses the offices of the provincial government, but you can visit

The Palazzo Medici-Riccardi

parts of it, notably the chapel and its **cycle of frescoes**, which a maximum of fifteen may view at any one time. To avoid the queues, book in advance at the ticket office, at Via Cavour 3, or call ⓣ 055 276 0340.

Painted around 1460, Benozzo Gozzoli's frescoes of *The Journey of the Magi* probably portray the pageant of the Compagnia dei Magi, the most patrician of the city's religious confraternities, whose annual procession took place at Epiphany. Several Medici were prominent members, including Piero de' Medici (Piero il Gottoso), who may have commissioned the pictures. It's known that several of the Medici household are featured in the procession, but putting names to these prettified faces is a problem. The man leading the cavalcade on a white horse is almost certainly Piero. Lorenzo il Magnifico, 11 years old at the time the fresco was painted, is probably the young king in the foreground, riding the grey horse detached from the rest of the procession, while his brother, Giuliano, is most likely the one preceded by the black bowman. The artist himself is in the crowd on the far left, his red beret signed with the words "Opus Benotii" in gold.

Another set of stairs leads up to the **first floor**, where a display case in the lobby of the main gallery contains a *Madonna and Child* (late 1460s) by Filippo Lippi. The ceiling of the grandiloquent **gallery** glows with Luca Giordano's fresco of *The Apotheosis of the Medici* (1683), from which one can only deduce that Giordano had no sense of shame. Accompanying Cosimo III on his flight into the ether is his son, the last male Medici, Gian Gastone, who grew to be a man so inert that he could rarely summon the energy to get out of bed in the morning.

The Mercato Centrale

MAP p.72, POCKET MAP D3
Piazza del Mercato Centrale (see p.86 for market opening times).

The Mercato Centrale was designed by Giuseppe Mengoni, architect of Milan's famous Galleria, and is one of Europe's largest covered food halls. Butchers, *alimentari*, tripe-sellers, greengrocers – they're all gathered under the one roof, along with some excellent *tavole calde* (of which *Nerbone* is the most famous), serving sandwiches and basic lunches. Opened in 1874, the Mercato Centrale received an overhaul a century later, reopening in 1980 with a new first floor; in 2014 another restoration transformed the upper level into a sort of indoor piazza with bars and eateries.

The San Lorenzo street market, which used to spread into Piazza San Lorenzo, is now confined to the streets surrounding the Mercato Centrale. Every day from 8am to 7pm this area is thronged with stalls selling bags, belts, leather jackets and football shirts. Quality isn't the highest, but prices are fairly low.

The Cenacolo di Fuligno

MAP p.72, POCKET MAP D3
Via Faenza 40. Tues, Thurs & Sat 9am–1pm. Donation requested.

Cenacoli (Last Suppers) were something of a Florentine artistic speciality, and there's a beguiling example of the genre – the *Cenacolo di Fuligno* – in the former Franciscan convent in Via Faenza. Discovered under layers of whitewash and grime in 1840, it was once thought to be by Raphael, then reassigned to Raphael's mentor Perugino. Latest research indicates that it was painted by Perugino's workshop but designed by the master in the 1490s. A small collection of contemporaneous devotional art hangs on the other walls of the former refectory.

The Mercato Centrale

The Fortezza da Basso

MAP p.72, POCKET MAP C1–C2
Piazza Adua.

The Fortezza da Basso was built to intimidate the people of Florence by the vile Alessandro de' Medici, who ordained himself duke of Florence after a ten-month siege by the army of Charles V and Pope Clement VII (possibly Alessandro's father) had forcibly restored the Medici. Within a few years the cruelties of Alessandro had become intolerable; a petition to Charles V spoke of the Fortezza da Basso as "a prison and a slaughterhouse for the unhappy citizens". Charles's response to Alessandro's atrocities was to marry his daughter to the tyrant. In the end, another Medici came to the rescue: in 1537 the distantly related Lorenzaccio de' Medici stabbed the duke to death. Subsequently the Fortezza da Basso fell into dereliction, but since 1978 it has been used for trade fairs and shows such as the Pitti Moda fashion jamborees in January and July; the city's main art-restoration workshops are here too.

The Cenacolo di Sant'Apollonia

MAP p.72, POCKET MAP E3
Via XXVII Aprile 1. Daily 8.15am–1.50pm;
closed 1st, 3rd & 5th Sun of month, and
2nd & 4th Mon. Free.

Most of the former Benedictine convent of Sant'Apollonia has now been turned into apartments, but the lower part of an entire wall of the former refectory is taken up with Andrea del Castagno's disturbing *Last Supper* (c.1447). Blood-red is the dominant tone, and the most commanding figure is the diabolic, black-bearded Judas, who sits on the near side of the table. The seething patterns in the marbled panels behind the Apostles seem to mimic the turmoil in the mind of each as he hears Christ's announcement of the betrayal. Castagno also painted the *Crucifixion*, *Deposition* and *Resurrection* above the illusionistic space in which the Last Supper takes place, and the *Crucifixion* and *Pietà* on the adjacent walls.

The Accademia

MAP p.72, POCKET MAP F3
Via Ricasoli 66 Ⓦ uffizi.firenze.it. Tues–Sun
8.15am–6.50pm. €8, or €12.50 during
special exhibitions.

The Galleria dell'Accademia has an extensive collection of paintings, but what draws the crowds is the sculpture of **Michelangelo**, in particular the *David*. So great is the public appetite for this one work in particular that you'd be well advised to book tickets in advance (see p.142).

Commissioned by the Opera del Duomo in 1501, the **David** was conceived to invoke parallels with Florence's recent liberation from Savonarola and the Medici. It's an incomparable show of technical bravura, all the more impressive given the difficulties posed by the marble from which it was carved. The four-metre block of stone – thin, shallow and riddled with cracks – had been quarried from Carrara forty years earlier. Several artists had already attempted to work with it, notably Leonardo da Vinci. Michelangelo succeeded where others had failed, completing the work in 1504 when he was still just 29. Displayed for almost four hundred years in the Piazza della Signoria, the *David* today occupies a specially built alcove, protected by a glass barrier that was built in 1991, after one of its toes was vandalized with a

Michelangelo's *David*

Michelangelo's *St Matthew*

Close by is another unfinished work, *St Matthew* (1505–06), started soon after completion of the *David* as a commission from the Opera del Duomo; they actually requested a full series of the Apostles from Michelangelo, but this is the only one he ever began.

The **picture galleries** that flank the main sculpture hall are generally unexciting, with copious examples of the work of "Unknown Florentine" and "Follower of …". The pieces likeliest to make an impact are Pontormo's *Venus and Cupid* (1532), painted to a cartoon by Michelangelo; a *Madonna of the Sea* (1470) attributed to Botticelli; and the painted fifteenth-century *Adimari Chest*, showing a Florentine wedding ceremony in the Piazza del Duomo.

hammer. In 2004 he was given a thorough cleaning for the first time in decades, restoring the gangly youth to something like his original brilliance.

Michelangelo once described the process of carving as being the liberation of the form from within the stone, a notion that seems to be embodied by the unfinished **Slaves** (or Prisoners). His procedure, clearly demonstrated here, was to cut the figure as if it were a deep relief, and then to free the three-dimensional figure; often his assistants would perform the initial operation, so it's possible that Michelangelo's own chisel never actually touched these stones. Probably carved in the late 1520s, the statues were originally destined for the tomb of Julius II, a project that was eventually abandoned; four of the original six statues came to the Accademia in 1909, while two others found their way to the Louvre.

The Museo dell'Opificio delle Pietre Dure

MAP p.72, POCKET MAP F3
Via degli Alfani 78. Mon–Sat 8.15am–2pm. €4.

Occupying a corner of the Accademia building, the Opificio delle Pietre Dure was founded in 1588 to train craftsmen in the distinctively Florentine art of creating pictures or patterns with highly polished, inlaid **semi-precious stones**. The museum clearly elucidates the highly skilled processes involved in the creation of *pietre dure* work, and has some remarkable examples of the genre. If you want to see some more spectacular (and rather gross) specimens, you should visit the Cappelle Medicee (see p.74). While local workshops still maintain the traditions of this specialized art-form, the Opificio itself has evolved into one of the world's leading centres for the restoration of artworks.

Fra' Angelico fresco, San Marco

The Museo di San Marco

MAP p.72, POCKET MAP F3

Piazza San Marco ⓦ uffizi.firenze.it. Tues–Fri 8.15am–1.50pm, Sat 8.15am–4.50pm, plus 1st, 3rd & 5th Mon of the month 8.15am–1.50pm, and 2nd & 4th Sun of the month 8.15am–4.50pm. €4.

Much of the north side of Piazza San Marco is taken up by the Dominican convent of San Marco, now the home of the Museo di San Marco. The Dominicans acquired the site in 1436, and the complex promptly became the recipient of Cosimo de' Medici's most lavish patronage. Ironically, the convent became the centre of resistance to the Medici later in the century: Girolamo Savonarola, leader of the government of Florence after the expulsion of the Medici in 1494, was the prior of San Marco.

During the Medici-funded rebuilding, the convent was decorated by one of its friars and a future prior, Fra' Angelico, a Tuscan painter in whom a medieval simplicity of faith was uniquely allied to a Renaissance sophistication of manner. Twenty or so paintings by the artist are gathered in the ground-floor **Ospizio dei Pellegrini**, or Pilgrims' Hospice, including several of Angelico's most famous creations. Here you'll see a wonderful *Deposition* that originally hung in the church of Santa Trìnita, the *Madonna dei Linaiuoli* (1433), which was Angelico's first major public painting, and the so-called *Pala di San Marco* (1440), a painting that has been badly damaged by the passage of time and a disastrous restoration, but demonstrates Fra' Angelico's familiarity with the principle of a central vanishing point, as expounded in Alberti's *Della Pittura* (*On Painting*), published in Italian just two years before the picture was executed.

Elsewhere on ground level you'll find Fra' Bartolomeo's portrait of Savonarola, his unfinished *Pala della Signoria*, and – in the **Sala Capitolare**, or Chapter House – a powerful fresco of the *Crucifixion*, painted by Angelico and assistants. Most of the main cloister's frescoes are sixteenth-century depictions of episodes from the life of Antonino Pierozzi, Fra' Angelico's mentor, who was canonized as St Antonine in 1523; Fra' Angelico himself painted the frescoes in its four corners. Before going upstairs, make sure you also see the **Refettorio Piccolo**, or Small Refectory, which has a lustrous *Last Supper* (1480) by Ghirlandaio.

At the top of the stairs you're confronted with one of the most sublime paintings in Italy: for the drama of its setting and the lucidity of its composition, nothing in San Marco matches Angelico's *Annunciation*. Angelico and his assistants also painted the simple and piously restrained pictures in each of the 44 **dormitory cells** on this floor, into which the friars would withdraw for solitary contemplation and sleep. Several of the scenes include one or both of a pair of monastic onlookers, serving as intermediaries between the occupant of the cell and the personages in the pictures: the one with the star above his head is St Dominic; the one with the split skull is St Peter Martyr.

The rooms once occupied by Savonarola now contain various relics questionably authenticated as worn by the man himself; the more luxuriously appointed cells 29 and 30 were the personal domain of Cosimo de' Medici – the fresco of the *Adoration of the Magi* may have been suggested by Cosimo himself, who liked to think of himself as a latter-day wise man and gift-giving king.

On the way to these VIP cells you'll pass the entrance to **Michelozzo's Library**, built in 1441–44 to a design that exudes an atmosphere of calm study. Cosimo's agents roamed as far as the Near East garnering precious manuscripts and books for him; in turn, Cosimo handed all the religious items over to the monastery, stipulating that they should be accessible to all, making this Europe's first **public library**. As the plaque by the doorway tells you, it was on this spot that Savonarola was arrested in 1498.

San Marco church

MAP p.72, POCKET MAP F3
Piazza San Marco. Mon–Sat 9.30am–noon & 4–5.30pm. Free.
The church of San Marco is worth a quick visit for two works on the second and third altars on the right: a *Madonna and Saints* painted in 1509 by Fra' Bartolomeo, and an eighth-century mosaic of *The Madonna in Prayer* (surrounded by later additions), brought here from Rome. This had to be cut in half in transit, and you can still see the break across the Virgin's midriff. The preserved body of St Antonine lies in a chapel designed by Giambologna, and the great Renaissance humanists Pico della Mirandola and Poliziano are entombed in the left wall of the nave, above the statue of Savonarola.

Main cloister, San Marco

The Chiostro dello Scalzo

MAP p.72, POCKET MAP F2
Via Cavour 69. Mon & Thurs
8.15am–1.50pm, plus first, third & fifth
Sat of the month and second & fourth Sun,
same hours. Free.

Lo Scalzo was the home of the
Brotherhood of St John, whose
vows of poverty entailed walking
around barefoot (*scalzo*). The
order was suppressed in 1785
and their monastery sold off,
except for the cloister, which was
the training ground for Andrea
del Sarto; his monochrome
paintings of *The Cardinal Virtues*
and *Scenes from the Life of the
Baptist* occupied him off and on
for a decade from 1511. A couple
of the sixteen scenes – *John in
the Wilderness* and *John meeting
Christ* – were executed by his
pupil Franciabigio in 1518, when
del Sarto was away in Paris.

The Giardino dei Semplici

The Giardino dei Semplici

MAP p.72, POCKET MAP F3
Via La Pira. April to mid-Oct Mon, Tues &
Thurs–Sun 10am–7pm; rest of year Sat &
Sun 10am–4pm. €3.

The Giardino dei Semplici or
Orto Botanico – the nearest
equivalent to the Bóboli garden
on the north side of the city –
was set up in 1545 for Cosimo I
as a **medicinal garden**, following
the examples of Padua and Pisa,
and now covers five acres, most
of the area being taken up by
the original flowerbeds and
avenues. The **university museums**
that adjoin the Giardino dei
Semplici – the Museo Botanico,
the Museo di Mineralogia e
Litologia and the Museo di
Geologia e Paleontologia – are of
specialist interest.

Piazza Santissima Annunziata

MAP p.72, POCKET MAP F3–F4

Nineteenth-century urban
renewal schemes left many
of Florence's squares rather
grim places, which makes the
pedestrianized Piazza Santissima
Annunziata, with its distinctive
arcades, all the more attractive
a public space. It has a special
importance for the city, too. Until
the end of the eighteenth century
the Florentine year used to
begin on March 25, the Festival
of the Annunciation – hence
the Florentine predilection for
paintings of the Annunciation,
and the fashionableness of the
Annunziata church, which
has long been the place for big
weddings. The festival is still
marked by a huge fair in the
piazza and the streets leading
off it; later in the year, on the
first weekend in September,
the square is used for Tuscany's
largest crafts fair.

  Brunelleschi began the piazza
in the 1420s, with additions
made later by Ammannati
and Antonio da Sangallo. The

equestrian statue of Grand Duke Ferdinando I (1608) at its centre was Giambologna's final work, and was cast by his pupil Pietro Tacca, from cannons captured at the Battle of Lepanto. Tacca was also the creator of the two bizarre **fountains**, on each of which a pair of aquatic monkeys spit water at two whiskered sea slugs.

The Spedale degli Innocenti

MAP p.72, POCKET MAP F4
Piazza Santissima Annunziata
Ⓦ istitutodeglinnocenti.it. Mon–Sat 10am–7pm, Sun 8.30am–2pm. €5.

Piazza Santissima Annunziata's most elegant building is the Spedale degli Innocenti, or Ospedale. Commissioned in 1419 by the Arte della Seta, the silk-weavers' guild, it opened in 1445 as the first foundlings' hospital in Europe, and is still an **orphanage** today. It was largely designed by Brunelleschi, and his nine-arched loggia was one of Europe's earliest examples of the new classically influenced style. (The building on the other side of the piazza was designed a century later, by Antonio da Sangallo and Baccio d'Agnolo, as accommodation for the Servite friars who staffed the orphanage.) Andrea della Robbia's blue-backed ceramic tondi of well-swaddled babies advertise the building's function, but their gaiety belies the misery associated with it. Slavery was part of the Florentine economy as late as the fifteenth century (it's probable that Leonardo da Vinci's mother was a slave), and many of the infants given to the care of the Spedale were born to domestic slaves. From 1660 children could be abandoned anonymously in the *rota*, a small revolving door whose bricked-up remains are still visible at the extreme left of the facade; it remained in use until 1875.

One of Tacca's fountains, Piazza Santissima Annunziata

The Museo degli Innocenti reopened in 2016 after a major renovation, and now comprises three sections. New exhibition space in the basement is devoted to the history and work of the Instituto degli Innocenti. On the ground floor, the focus is on two beautiful cloisters, Brunelleschi's Cortile degli Uomini (Men's Court) and the graceful Cortile delle Donne (Women's Court). Upstairs, the gallery contains a miscellany of Florentine Renaissance art that includes one of Luca della Robbia's most beguiling Madonnas and an *Adoration of the Magi* (1488) by Domenico Ghirlandaio. The smartened-up Spedale now has a café on the top floor, with a panoramic terrace.

Piazza Santissima Annunziata

Santissima Annunziata

MAP p.72, POCKET MAP F3
Piazza Santissima Annunziata. Daily
7.30am–12.30pm & 4–6.30pm. Free.

Santissima Annunziata is the
mother church of the **Servites**,
or Servi di Maria (Servants of
Mary), a religious order founded
by Filippo Benizzi and six
Florentine aristocrats in 1234.
From humble beginnings, the
order blossomed after 1252,
when a painting of the Virgin
begun by one of the monks but
abandoned in despair because
of his inability to create a truly
beautiful image, was supposedly
completed by an angel while he
slept. So many people came to
venerate the image that by 1444
a new church, financed by the
Medici, was commissioned from
Michelozzo, who happened to
be the brother of the Servites'
head prior.

   As the number of pilgrims
to the church increased, so it
became a custom to leave wax
votive offerings (*voti*) in honour

of its miraculous Madonna.
These became so numerous
that in 1447 a special atrium,
the **Chiostrino dei Voti**, was
built onto the church, and in
1516 a major fresco cycle was
commissioned, on the occasion
of the canonization of Filippo
Benizzi. Three leading artists of
the day, Andrea del Sarto, Jacopo
Pontormo and Rosso Fiorentino,
were involved, together with
several lesser painters. Some of
the panels are in a poor state – all
were removed from the walls
and restored after the 1966 flood
(see box, p.94) – but their overall
effect is superb.

   Just inside the church itself,
on the left, stands the ornate
tabernacle (1448–61) designed
by Michelozzo to house the
miraculous image of the
Madonna. The nearby **Cappella
Feroni** features a fresco by
Andrea del Castagno of *Christ
and St Julian* (1455–56); a more
striking fresco by the same
artist, *The Holy Trinity and St
Jerome* (1454), can be seen in the
adjacent chapel. Now restored,
both frescoes were obliterated
after Vasari spread the rumour
that Castagno had poisoned
his erstwhile friend, Domenico
Veneziano, motivated by envy
of the other's skill with oil paint.
Castagno was saddled with
this crime until the nineteenth
century, when an archivist
discovered that the alleged
murderer in fact predeceased his
victim by four years. The church's
other notable painting is Andrea
del Sarto's intimate *Madonna
del Sacco* (1525) in the spacious
Chiostro dei Morti, over the
door that opens from the north
transept (you may need to find
the sacristan to open it); the
picture – more formally known
as *Rest during the Flight into
Egypt* – takes its curious name
from the sack on which St Joseph
is leaning.

The Museo Archeologico

MAP p.72, POCKET MAP F3–G4
Via della Colonna 36 Ⓦ archeotoscana
.beniculturali.it. Mon, Sat & Sun
8.30am–2pm, Tues–Fri 8.30am–7pm. €4.

The special strength of the Museo Archeologico is its **Etruscan** collection, much of it bequeathed, inevitably, by the Medici. Most of the finds are on the first floor, where there's a large array of funerary figures and two outstanding bronze sculptures: the *Arringatore* (Orator), the only known large Etruscan bronze from the Hellenistic period, made some time around 100 BC; and the *Chimera*, a triple-headed monster made in the fourth century BC.

Numerous dowdy cabinets are stuffed with unlabelled Etruscan figurines, and much of the **Egyptian collection** is displayed in a similarly uninspiring manner. The single most remarkable object amid the assembly of papyri, statuettes and mummy cases is a Hittite chariot made of bone and wood, dating from the fourteenth century BC.

There are more Etruscan pieces on the top floor (sometimes open only to guided tours), but here the primary focus is on the **Greek and Roman collections**. The star piece in the huge hoard of Greek vases is the large *François Vase*, a sixth-century BC *krater*. Another attention-grabbing item is the life-size bronze torso known as the *Torso di Livorno*, either a fifth-century BC Greek original or a Roman copy. There's some debate also about the large horse's head that's on show in the same room. This fragment of a full-size statue is probably an early Hellenistic bronze from around 100 BC, but again it may be a Roman copy; what's known for certain is that it was once in the garden of the Palazzo Medici, where it was studied by Donatello and Verrocchio. Also on this floor you'll see two beautiful sixth-century BC Greek *kouroi*, dubbed *Apollo* and *Apollino*, and the bronze statue of a young man known as the *Idolino di Pésaro* – it's generally thought to be a Roman replica of a Greek figure dating from around 100 BC.

The *Chimera* in the Museo Archeologico

Shops & markets

Alinari

MAP p.72, POCKET MAP D4
Largo Alinari 15 ☎ 055 239 51, ⓦ alinari
.com. Tues–Sun 10am–6pm; closed 2 weeks
in mid-Aug.

Established in 1852, this is the world's oldest photographic business. Owners of the best archive of vintage photographs in Italy, they will print any image you choose from their huge catalogue. They also publish books, calendars, posters and cards.

Mercato Centrale

MAP p.72, POCKET MAP D3
Piazza del Mercato Centrale. Daily
8pm–midnight.

The vast food hall is great for picnic supplies, but well worth a sightseeing and people-watching visit whether you intend to buy anything or not. *Nerbone*, one of the market's excellent *tavole calde*, serves meatballs, pasta, stews, soups, salads and sandwiches – perfect for a simple but hearty lunch. The upper floor of the market, which reopened in 2014 after a major renovation, has a pizzeria, a birreria, a wine bar and various other places to eat and drink, which keep the building lively long after the market stalls have shut down for the day.

San Lorenzo market

MAP p.72, POCKET MAP D4
Piazza di San Lorenzo. Daily 9am–7pm.

A vast open-air warehouse of cheap clothing, bags and belts. If you're looking for a low-price replica Fiorentina shirt or a bargain leather jacket, this is the place.

Cafés & bars

Casa del Vino

MAP p.72, POCKET MAP D4
Via dell'Ariento 16r ☎ 055 215 609. Oct–
May Mon–Thurs 9.30am–3.30pm, Fri & Sat
10am–10pm; June, July & Sept closed Sat;
closed all Aug.

Located a few yards from the Mercato Centrale, this wine bar is thronged at lunchtime with traders who pitch up for a drink, a chat with owner Gianni Migliorini and a few *panini* or *crostini*.

La Ménagère

MAP p.72, POCKET MAP E4
Via de' Ginori 8r ☎ 055 075 0600,
ⓦ lamenagere.it. Daily 7am–2am.

Formerly a market hall, this building has been spectacularly refashioned as a bar-bistro-restaurant-café, with a home accessories boutique and a florist on the premises too. Rusty tables and unplastered walls set a tone of distressed chic, and the vaulted dining room, with its single 18-metre table, is amazing. *La Ménagère* is perhaps best, however, as a place for a morning coffee, a light lunch or a late-night drink.

Robiglio

MAP p.72, POCKET MAP F4
Via dei Servi 112r ☎ 055 214 501. Daily
8am–8pm.

Handbags for sale, San Lorenzo market

Robiglio

Renowned for its pastries and chocolates, *Robiglio* also makes good ice cream and specializes in a hot chocolate drink that's so thick it's barely a liquid. Founded here in 1928, *Robiglio* now has four other branches, the most central of which is at Via Tosinghi 11r, near the Duomo.

Zanobini

MAP p.72, POCKET MAP D4
Via Sant'Antonino 47r ☎ 055 239 6850.
Mon–Sat 8am–2pm & 3.30–8pm.

Like the nearby *Casa del Vino* this is an authentic and long-established place, but here the emphasis is more on the wine: few bars in Florence have a better selection.

Gelateria

Carabé

MAP p.72, POCKET MAP E4
Via Ricasoli 60r ☎ 055 289 476.
April–Oct daily 10am–1am; Nov–March 10am–8pm, but closed mid-Dec to mid-Jan.

Wonderful Sicilian ice cream made with Sicilian ingredients as only they know how. Try the *Spirito Siciliano* flavour – the most lemony lemon you'll ever taste. Also serves delicious *cannoli* (pastry stuffed with sweet ricotta and candied fruits).

Restaurants

Da Mario

MAP p.72, POCKET MAP E3
Via Rosina 2r ☎ 055 218 550,
🌐 trattoria-mario.com. Mon–Sat noon–3.30pm; closed Aug.

For earthy Florentine cooking at low prices, there's nowhere better than *Da Mario*, which has been in operation since 1953. It's just a pity it isn't open in the evenings. No credit cards; no booking.

Sergio Gozzi

MAP p.72, POCKET MAP E4
Piazza San Lorenzo 8r ☎ 055 281 941.
Mon–Sat 11am–3pm.

This plain bar-trattoria, lurking behind the San Lorenzo market stalls, is a good choice for an inexpensive lunch, with a short and simple menu that changes daily. It does not take reservations.

Zà–Zà

MAP p.72, POCKET MAP E3
Piazza del Mercato Centrale 26r ☎ 055 215 411, 🌐 trattoriazaza.it. Daily 11am–11pm; closed Aug.

In business for more than forty years, *Zà–Zà* has become a guidebook mainstay, and it's still one of the best *trattorias* close to the Mercato Centrale. The menu has lots of salads, seafood dishes and Tuscan meats; expect to pay around €12–20 for a main course.

East of the centre

The vast Franciscan church of Santa Croce is one of the most compelling sights in Florence, and forms the centrepiece of an area which, prior to the terrible flood of 1966, was one of the city's more densely populated districts. When the Arno burst its banks, this low-lying quarter, packed with tenements and small workshops, was virtually wrecked, and many of its residents moved out permanently in the following years. Now, however, the district has revived in a big way, and it's here that you'll find many of the city's liveliest bars and best restaurants. In addition to the mighty Santa Croce, the district's cultural attractions are the Museo Horne, the Casa Buonarroti, and a brace of smaller churches.

Santa Croce

MAP p.90, POCKET MAP F6–G6
Piazza Santa Croce Ⓦ santacroceopera.it.
Mon–Sat 9.30am–5.30pm, Sun 2–5.30pm. €8.

The church of Santa Croce is the Franciscans' principal church in Florence and is said to have been founded by St Francis himself. In truth it was probably begun seventy or so years after Francis's death, in 1294, possibly by the architect of the Duomo,

Arnolfo di Cambio. Ironically, it was the city's richest families who funded the construction of the church: plutocrats such as the Bardi, Peruzzi and Baroncelli sponsored the extraordinary **fresco cycles** that were lavished on the chapels over the years, particularly during the fourteenth century, when artists of the stature of Giotto and the Gaddi family worked

Primo Chiostro, Santa Croce

here. And Santa Croce has long served as the national pantheon: it contains monuments to more than 270 illustrious Italians, including Michelangelo, Galileo, Machiavelli and Dante (though the last is not buried here).

On your way to the frescoed chapels be sure to take a look at Donatello's gilded stone relief of the *Annunciation* (against the right-hand wall) and Bernardo Rossellino's nearby tomb of Leonardo Bruni, chancellor of the Republic, humanist scholar and author of the first history of the city. (His successor as chancellor, Carlo Marsuppini, is commemorated by a splendid tomb in the opposite aisle, carved by Desiderio da Settignano.) The **Cappella Castellani**, at the end of the south aisle, was strikingly frescoed by Agnolo Gaddi and his pupils, while the adjoining **Cappella Baroncelli** was decorated by Agnolo's father, Taddeo, a long-time assistant to Giotto.

Both the **Cappella Peruzzi** and the **Cappella Bardi** – the two chapels on the right of the chancel – are covered with frescoes by Giotto, with some assistance in the latter. Their deterioration was partly caused by Giotto's having painted some of the pictures onto dry plaster, but the vandalism of later generations was far more destructive. Scenes from the lives of St John the Evangelist and St John the Baptist fill the Peruzzi chapel, while a better-preserved cycle of the life of St Francis fills the Bardi. Despite the areas of paint destroyed when a tomb was attached to the wall, the *Funeral of St Francis* is still a composition of extraordinary impact, the grief-stricken mourners suggesting an affinity with the lamentation over the body of Christ – one of them even probes the wound in Francis's side, echoing the gesture of Doubting Thomas.

Santa Croce

From the right transept a corridor leads to the **Cappella Medici**, which contains Bronzino's huge *Descent of Christ into Limbo* and an altarpiece by Andrea and Giovanni della Robbia. Adjoining the corridor, the beautifully panelled sacristy is home to Cimabue's great *Crucifix*, which was half-destroyed in the 1966 flood and has become in effect the emblem of that disaster.

On the other side of the church there's a second **Cappella Bardi**, which houses a wooden crucifix by Donatello, supposedly criticized by Brunelleschi as resembling a "peasant on the Cross".

The door in the right aisle leads through into the church's Primo Chiostro (First Cloister), site of Brunelleschi's **Cappella Pazzi**, the epitome of the learned, harmonious spirit of early Renaissance architecture, with lovely terracotta work by Luca della Robbia and his workshop.

The **Museo dell'Opera di Santa Croce**, flanking the first cloister, houses a miscellany of works, including Donatello's gilded *St Louis of Toulouse* (1424). Next door is the serene **Inner Cloister**, another late project by Brunelleschi.

East of the centre

Casa Buonarroti

MAP p.90, POCKET MAP G6
Via Ghibellina 70 ⓦ casabuonarroti.it.
Mon & Wed–Sun 10am–5pm (4pm in
winter). €6.50.

The enticing name of the
Casa Buonarroti is somewhat
misleading: **Michelangelo
Buonarroti** certainly owned three
houses here in 1508, and probably
lived on the site intermittently
between 1516 and 1525, but
on Michelangelo's death they
passed to his nephew, whose
son converted them into a single
palazzo, leaving little trace of the
earlier houses. Michelangelo's
last descendant, Cosimo, left the
building to the city on his death
in 1858. Today the house contains
a smart but low-key **museum**,
nicely decorated in period style
and adorned with beautiful
furniture, objets d'art, frescoed
ceilings and the like, but only a
handful of the works of art on

display are by Michelangelo. The
Madonna della Scala (c.1490–92)
is Michelangelo's earliest known
work, a delicate relief carved
when he was no older than 16.
The similarly unfinished *Battle of
the Centaurs* was created shortly
afterwards, when he was living
in the Medici household. In the
adjacent room you'll find the
artist's wooden model (1517) for
the facade of San Lorenzo, close
to the largest of all the sculptural
models on display, the torso of a
River God (1524), a work probably
intended for the Medici chapel
in San Lorenzo. Other rooms
contain small and fragmentary
pieces, possibly by the master,
possibly copies of works by him.

Sant'Ambrogio

MAP p.90, POCKET MAP H5
Piazza di Sant'Ambrogio. Daily 8am–12.30pm
& 4–7pm. Free.

Sant'Ambrogio is one of
Florence's oldest churches,

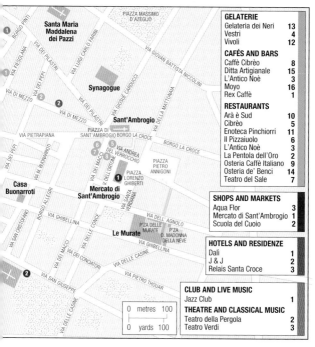

GELATERIE

Gelateria dei Neri	13
Vestri	4
Vivoli	12

CAFÉS AND BARS

Caffè Cibrèo	8
Ditta Artigianale	15
L'Antico Noè	3
Moyo	16
Rex Caffè	1

RESTAURANTS

Arà è Sud	10
Cibrèo	5
Enoteca Pinchiorri	11
Il Pizzaiuolo	6
L'Antico Noè	3
La Pentola dell'Oro	2
Osteria Caffè Italiano	9
Osteria de' Benci	14
Teatro del Sale	7

SHOPS AND MARKETS

Aqua Flor	3
Mercato di Sant'Ambrogio	1
Scuola del Cuoio	2

HOTELS AND RESIDENZE

Dalì	1
J & J	2
Relais Santa Croce	3

CLUB AND LIVE MUSIC

Jazz Club	1

THEATRE AND CLASSICAL MUSIC

Teatro della Pergola	2
Teatro Verdi	3

having been documented in 988, though rebuilding over the centuries has resulted in a somewhat bland appearance. Inside you'll find a *Madonna Enthroned with SS John the Baptist and Bartholomew* (second altar on the right), attributed to Orcagna (or the school of Orcagna), and a recently restored triptych in the chapel to the right of the main altar, attributed to Lorenzo di Bicci or Bicci di Lorenzo. More compelling than either painting, though, is the **Cappella del Miracolo**, the chapel to the left of the high altar, and its tabernacle (1481–83) by Mino da Fiesole, an accomplished sculptor whose name crops up time and again across Tuscany. This was one of Mino's last works – he died in 1484 – making it fitting that he should be buried close by, in a pavement tomb at the chapel entrance.

(Another great artist, Verrocchio, who died in 1488, is buried in the fourth chapel.)

The narrative fresco (1486) alongside the tabernacle alludes to the miracle which gave the Cappella del Miracolo its name. The work of Cosimo Rosselli (best known for his frescoes in Santissima Annunziata), it depicts a procession bearing a chalice in which, during a Mass conducted here in 1230, the communion wine was discovered to have turned into blood. The Florentines believed the chalice saved them from, among other things, the effects of a plague outbreak of 1340. The painting is full of portraits of Rosselli's contemporaries, making it another of Florence's vivid pieces of Renaissance social reportage: Rosselli himself is the figure in the black beret at the extreme left of the picture.

The Synagogue

MAP p.90, POCKET MAP G5
Via Farini 4. Sun–Thurs 10am–5.30pm, Fri
10am–3pm. €6.50.

The enormous domed building rising to the north of Sant'Ambrogio church is the Synagogue; the ghetto established in this district by Cosimo I was not demolished until the second half of the nineteenth century, which is when the present Moorish-style synagogue was built. It contains a **museum** that charts the history of Florence's Jewish population.

Santa Maria Maddalena dei Pazzi

MAP p.90, POCKET MAP G4
Borgo Pinti. Church Mon–Sat
8am–12.30pm & 4–7pm, Sun
8am–12.30pm. Perugino fresco Tues &
Thurs 2.30–5.30pm. Free.

The church of Santa Maria Maddalena dei Pazzi is named named after a Carmelite nun – a member of the clan who murdered Giuliano de' Medici (see box, p.30) – who was famed for her healing powers

The Synagogue

and religious ecstasies: when possessed by the spirit she would spew words at such a rate that a team of eight novices was needed to transcribe her inspired dictation. She was also prone to pouring boiling wax over her arms, and was fond of reclining naked on a bed of thorns. Such fervent piety was much honoured in Counter-Reformation Florence, and a cult grew up around her immediately after her death in 1607; canonisation followed in 1669.

Founded in the thirteenth century, the church is fronted by a lovely courtyard designed by Giuliano da Sangallo. Inside, paintings celebrating St Maria – including a pair by Luca Giordano – adorn the marble-clad chancel. In contrast to all this Baroque fervour, the convent's chapterhouse – entered via a doorway at Via della Colonna 9 – is decorated with a radiant **Perugino** fresco of the *Crucifixion*. Based on the terrain around Lago Trasimeno, the scene is painted as a continuous panorama on a wall divided into three arches, giving the effect of looking out through a loggia onto a springtime landscape. As always with Perugino, there is nothing troubling here, the Crucifixion being depicted not as an agonizing death but rather as the necessary prelude to the Resurrection.

The English Cemetery

MAP p.90, POCKET MAP H3
Piazza Donatello. Daily 9am–noon &
3–6pm.

North of the Pazzi church, at the end of Borgo Pinti, lies the English Cemetery. Now stranded amid the traffic, this patch of garden is the resting place of Elizabeth Barrett Browning and a number of contemporaneous artistic Brits, among them Walter Savage Landor and Arthur Hugh Clough.

Sant'ambrogio

The Museo Horne

MAP p.90, POCKET MAP F7
**Via de' Benci 6 Ⓦ museohorne.it. Mon, Tues
& Thurs–Sun 10am–2pm. €7.**
On the south side of Santa
Croce, not far from the river,
stands one of Florence's more
recondite museums, the Museo
della Fondazione Horne. Its
collection was left to the state by
the English art historian Herbert
Percy Horne (1864–1916), who
was instrumental in rescuing
Botticelli from neglect with a
pioneering biography that was
published in 1908. The half-dozen
rooms of paintings, sculptures,
pottery, furniture and other
domestic objects contain few
masterpieces, but are diverting
enough if you've already done the
major collections.

The museum building, the
fifteenth-century **Palazzo
Corsi-Alberti**, is worth a look
even if you're not going into
the museum. Commissioned
by the Corsi family, it's a typical
merchant's house of the period,
with huge cellars in which wool
would have been dyed, and an
open gallery above the courtyard
for drying the finished cloth.

The pride of Horne's collection
was its drawings, which are
now salted away in the Uffizi,
though a small selection is often
displayed on the **ground floor**.
On the first floor, Room 1 has
pictures by Filippino Lippi and
Piero di Cosimo, an unfinished
and age-darkened *Deposition* by
Gozzoli (his last documented
work), a tiny and badly damaged
panel by Masaccio, showing
Scenes from the Life of St Julian,
and a terracotta *Venus* by
Giambologna. The next room
contains the collection's big draw,
Giotto's *St Stephen* (a fragment
from a polyptych), which was
probably painted at around the
time that Giotto was at work
in Santa Croce. Room 3 has a
tondo of the *Holy Family* by
Beccafumi, who is also attributed
with a *Drunkenness of Noah* on
the **second floor**, where you'll
find small works by Filippo and
Filippino Lippi, and a portable
diptych by Simone Martini and
Lippo Memmi.

Florence's floods

Calamitous floods are nothing new in Florence. Great areas of the city were destroyed by floodwater in 1178, and in 1269 the Carraia and Trìnita bridges were carried away on a torrent so heavy that "a great part of the city of Florence became a lake", as a contemporary chronicler put it. Bridges were also destroyed by the raging Arno in 1333, and Cosimo I instituted an urban beautification scheme after a flood put nearly twenty feet of muddy water over parts of the city in 1557; on that occasion the Trìnita bridge was hit so suddenly that everyone

The Cimabue Crucifix at Santa Croce

on it was drowned, except for a couple of children who were left stranded on a pillar in midstream, where for two days they were fed by means of a rope slung over from the bank.

It rained continuously for forty days prior to November 4, **1966**, with nearly half a metre of rain falling in the preceding two days. When the water pressure in an upstream reservoir threatened to break the dam, it was decided to open the sluices. The only people to be warned about the rapidly rising level of the river were the jewellers of the Ponte Vecchio, whose private nightwatchman phoned them in the small hours of the morning with news that the bridge was starting to shake. When the banks of the Arno finally broke, a flash flood dumped around 500,000 tonnes of water and mud on the streets, moving with such speed that people were drowned in the underpass of Santa Maria Novella train station. In all, 35 Florentines were killed, 6000 shops put out of business, more than 10,000 homes made uninhabitable, some 15,000 cars wrecked, and thousands of works of art damaged, many of them ruined by heating oil flushed out of basements.

Within hours an impromptu army of rescue workers had been formed to haul pictures out of slime-filled churches and gather fragments of paint in plastic bags. Donations came in from all over the world, but the task was so immense that the restoration of many items is still continuing – scores of precious books from the National Library, which is located next door to Santa Croce and took the brunt of the flood, remain in the laboratories. In total around two-thirds of the 3000 paintings damaged in the flood are now on view again (including the great **Cimabue Crucifix**, pictured, which has become an emblem of the disaster), and two laboratories – one for paintings and one for stonework – are operating full time in Florence, developing restoration techniques that are taken up by galleries all over the world. Today, throughout the city, you can see small marble plaques with a red line showing the level the floodwaters reached on that dreadful day in 1966.

Shops & markets

Aqua Flor

MAP p.90, POCKET MAP F6
Borgo Santa Croce 6 ☎ 055 234 3471,
🌐 florenceparfum.com. Daily 10am–7pm.
Master perfumer Sileno Cheloni
has a "library" of some 1500
natural ingredients, gathered from
all over the world, with which to
create a range of fragrances that
are unique to this atelier. Off-
the-peg perfumes are €120–180
(bespoke scents are much more);
soaps from just €10.

Mercato di Sant'Ambrogio

MAP p.90, POCKET MAP H5
Piazza Sant'Ambrogio. Mon–Sat 7am–2pm.
Out of the orbit of most tourists,
the Mercato di Sant'Ambrogio
is a smaller, tattier but equally
enjoyable version of the San
Lorenzo food hall. The *tavola
calda* is one of Florence's
lunchtime bargains, and – as at
San Lorenzo – the stalls bring
their prices down in the last hour
of trading.

Scuola del Cuoio

MAP p.90, POCKET MAP G6
Via San Giuseppe 5r ☎ 055 244 533,
🌐 scuoladelcuoio.com. Summer daily
10am–6pm; winter closed Sun.
This academy for leather-workers
sells bags, jackets, belts and other
accessories at prices that compare
very favourably with the shops. You
won't find any startlingly original
designs here, but the quality is
very high and the staff are both
knowledgeable and helpful.

Gelaterie

Gelateria dei Neri

MAP p.90, POCKET MAP F6
Via dei Neri 9–11r. Daily 10am–midnight.
Located close to Santa Croce, Dei
Neri serves what many think is the
best ice cream in town. The range
of flavours is fantastic – fig and

Scuola del Cuoio

walnut, Mexican chocolate (very
spicy), rice – and they have some
dairy-free ice cream too.

Vestri

MAP p.90, POCKET MAP F5
Piazza Gaetano Salvemini 11r ☎ 055 234
0374, 🌐 vestri.it. Mon–Sat 10.30am–8pm.
Chocoholics should make a bee-
line for Vestri, where ice cream
is just one of the concoctions on
offer – there's also deliciously thick
drinking chocolate and a mouth-
watering array of sweets and other
chocolate products. The ice cream
comes in a dozen flavours, but the
cocoa-based stuff is what they are
renowned for.

Vivoli

MAP p.90, POCKET MAP F6
Via Isola delle Stinche 7r. Tues–Sat
7.30am–midnight, Sun 9am–midnight;
closed 2 weeks in Aug.
Operating from deceptively
ordinary premises in a side street
close to Santa Croce, this has long
been rated one of the best ice-
cream-makers in Florence – and
some say in all of Italy.

Cafés & bars

Caffè Cibrèo

MAP p.90, POCKET MAP G5
Via Andrea del Verrocchio 5r ☎ 055 234
5853. Mon–Fri noon–11pm, Sat
8am–11pm; closed 2 weeks in Aug.

Possibly the prettiest café in
Florence, with a chi-chi clientele
to match. Opened in 1989, the
wood-panelled interior looks at
least two hundred years older.
Cakes and desserts are great, and
the light meals bear the culinary
stamp of the *Cibrèo* restaurant
kitchens opposite.

Ditta Artigianale

MAP p.90, POCKET MAP D13
Via dei Neri 32 🌐 dittaartigianale.it. Sun–
Thurs 8am–1pm, Fri 8am–midnight, Sat
9.30am–midnight.

The *Artigianale* has been in
business since 2013 and is
probably Florence's coolest
new café. It might be a bit
too self-consciously hip, but
the coffee is terrific – they
showcase a different roast
every month. And it does look
very good; the architects who
designed it were also responsible
for the spectacular *La Ménagère*
(see p.86).

L'Antico Noè

MAP p.90, POCKET MAP F5
Volta di San Piero 6r. Mon–Sat noon–3pm
& 7pm–midnight.

The "Old Noah" is a long-
established and utterly authentic
stand-up wine bar, tucked into
an uninviting little alley to the
north of Santa Croce, at the
end of Borgo Albizi. Excellent
sandwiches and other snacks.

Moyo

MAP p.90, POCKET MAP F6
Via de' Benci 23r ☎ 055 247 9738,
🌐 moyo.it. Daily 8am–3am, Fri & Sat
8am–3am.

A young crowd flocks to this bar
every evening – the food's pretty
good (come for the early-evening
aperitivo buffet) and the free wi-fi
access is a plus, but it's the buzz
that really brings them in. There's
a DJ set on Monday, Wednesday
and Thursday – everything from
Latin to hip-hop.

Rex Caffè

MAP p.90, POCKET MAP G5
Via Fiesolana 25r ☎ 055 248 0331. Daily
6pm–3am; closed June–Aug.

One of the city's real night-time
fixtures, this is a friendly bar-club
with a varied and loyal clientele.
Vast curving lights droop over the

Rex Caffè

central bar, which is studded with turquoise stone and broken mirror mosaics. Big arched spaces to either side mean there's plenty of room, the cocktails are good and the snacks excellent. DJs provide the sounds at weekends.

Restaurants

Arà è Sud

MAP p.90, POCKET MAP F6
Via della Vigna Vecchia 4r ☏ 331 217 0926, ⓦ araristorante.it. Mon & Wed–Sun 12.30–3pm & 7–11pm.

An offshoot and near neighbour of *Caffè Italiano*, this slick little bistro offers a menu that's small but quite unlike any other restaurant in Florence – the dishes are inspired by southern Italy and Sicily, with fish and seafood a strong presence. Mains average around €15.

Cibrèo

MAP p.90, POCKET MAP G5
Via de' Macci 118r ☏ 055 234 1100, ⓦ cibreo.com. Tues–Sun 12.30–2.30pm & 7–11.15pm; closed Aug.

Fabio Picchi's *Cibrèo* is the first Florentine port-of-call for many foodies, having achieved fame well beyond the city. The recipe for success is simple: superb food with a creative take on Tuscan classics, served in a tastefully neo-traditional dining room by friendly staff. You'll need to book days in advance for a table in the main part of the restaurant, but next door there's *Cibreino*, a small trattoria section where the food is of identical quality (though the menu is smaller), no bookings are taken and the prices are lower: around €15 for the main course; it's nearly €40 in the restaurant.

Enoteca Pinchiorri

MAP p.90, POCKET MAP F6
Via Ghibellina 87 ☏ 055 242 777, ⓦ enotecapinchiorri.it. Tues 7.30–10pm, Thurs–Sat 12.30–2pm & 7.30–10pm; closed Aug.

Cibrèo

This is the only Tuscan restaurant to have been given three Michelin stars, and no one seriously disputes *Pinchiorri*'s claim to be Florence's best restaurant. The food is as magnificent as the plaudits suggest, but the formality of the place is not to everyone's taste. The prices are delirious: pasta dishes can cost as much as €75, main courses around €90, while the ever-changing set menus cost around €250 per person, wine excluded – though you may get as many as twenty exquisite little dishes in the *menu degustazione*. The wine list has no equal in Italy, with some 150,000 bottles lying in the *Pinchiorri* cellars; bottles start at about €80, rising to five-figure sums.

Il Pizzaiuolo

MAP p.90, POCKET MAP G5
Via de' Macci 113r ☏ 055 241 171, ⓦ ilpizzaiuolo.it. Mon–Sat 12.30–2.30pm & 7.30pm–midnight; closed Aug.

The Neapolitan pizzas here are among the best in the city (there are thirty varieties on offer), and the rest of the menu has a Neapolitan touch too – as does the atmosphere, which is high-spirited. The wine list, as you might expect, is full of southern Italian vintages rather than the usual Tuscans. Reservations advisable in the evening.

L'Antico Noè

MAP p.90, POCKET MAP F5
Volta di San Piero 6r ☏ 055 234 0838.
Mon–Sat 12.30, 3pm & 7–11pm, Sun
12.30–3pm.

Situated next door to the excellent
vinaio of the same name (see
p.96), this tiny and long-
established trattoria is one for
hard-core carnivores – plate-filling
slabs of prime-quality grilled meat
are the only *secondi* on offer. The
decor is plain (you sit on wicker-
seated stools) but the prices are
not – expect to pay upward of €25
for your steak.

La Pentola dell'Oro

MAP p.90, POCKET MAP G5
Via di Mezzo 24r ☏ 055 241 808. Mon–Sat
12.30–2.30pm & 7.30–10.30pm, Sun
7.30–10.30pm.

La Pentola has one of the more
imaginative menus in Florence,
mingling the innovative with the
profoundly traditional. Some
of the recipes used by head chef
Giuseppe Alessi date back as far as
the fourteenth century, and there
are three different types of *bistecca*
on offer. Most main courses are

less than €15, which is more
than reasonable for cooking of
this quality, even if the basement
dining room isn't the most
comfortable in the city.

Osteria Caffè Italiano

MAP p.90, POCKET MAP F6
Via Isola delle Stinche 11–13r ☏ 055 289
020, ⓦ caffeitaliano.it. Daily 12.30–2.30pm
& 7–11pm.

The vaulted and cabinet-lined
main room of this upmarket
café-wine bar-restaurant is one of
the best-looking in Florence, and
the food more than lives up to the
setting. The cuisine is typically
Tuscan – lots of beef, veal and wild
boar – and first-rate; main courses
cost around €20. In the evening,
wood-oven pizzas are served in a
small room next door.

Osteria de' Benci

MAP p.90, POCKET MAP F6
Borgo Santa Croce 31r ☏ 055 234 4923,
ⓦ osteriadeibenci.it. Daily 12.30–2.30pm
& 7.30–11pm.

The dining room of this
modern and popular *osteria* is
augmented by outside tables in

Osteria Caffè Italiano

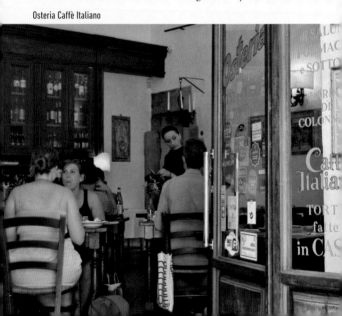

summer, and the moderately priced menu (mains around €15) consists of well-prepared standards plus innovative takes on Tuscan classics.

Teatro del Sale

MAP p.90, POCKET MAP G5
Via dei Macci 111r ☎ 055 200 1492,
Ⓦ teatrodelsale.com. Tues–Sat 9am–3pm & 6pm–midnight.

Run by Fabio Picchi, the boss of *Cibrèo* (see p.97), this unique place is a combination of restaurant and cultural centre. You pay €7 annual membership (valid for one guest too), and then an extra amount to help yourself to the amazing buffets: €7 for breakfast (9–11am), €15–20 for lunch (noon–2.15pm), and €30 for dinner (7–9pm), when Picchi himself is often on duty in the open kitchen, announcing the dishes as they're put out. At 9.45pm, guests are treated to a show, which might be anything from stand-up comedy to a piano recital or a dance group. If you don't want to eat, you can just hang out, drink coffee and browse through the books and magazines that are lying around. Needless to say, it's very popular, and reservations are advisable in the evenings.

Clubs & live music

Jazz Club

MAP p.90, POCKET MAP G4
Via Nuova de' Caccini 3 ☎ 055 247 9700.
Tues–Thurs & Sun 11pm–3am, Fri–Sat 11pm–4am; closed July & Aug.

Florence's foremost jazz venue. The €6 "membership" fee gets you down into the medieval brick-vaulted basement, where the atmosphere's informal and there's live music nearly every night (and an open jam-session on Tuesdays). Cocktails are good (if expensive), and you can also snack on bar nibbles, *focaccia* and desserts.

Theatre & classical music

Teatro della Pergola

MAP p.90, POCKET MAP F5
Via della Pergola 18 ☎ 055 226 4316,
Ⓦ teatrodellapergola.com.

The beautiful little Pergola was built in 1656 and is Italy's oldest surviving theatre. It plays host to top-flight instrumental recitals, chamber concerts and some of the best-known Italian theatre companies. The theatre season runs from October to April, and during the Maggio Musicale the Pergola is often used for small-scale operas.

Teatro Verdi

MAP p.90, POCKET MAP F6
Via Ghibellina 99–101 ☎ 055 212 320,
Ⓦ teatroverdionline.it.

Home to the Orchestra della Toscana, the Teatro Verdi is one of the city's premier venues for classical music, musicals and mainstream theatre productions. It hosts rock bands occasionally too.

Le Murate

The former prison of Le Murate (Ⓦ lemurate.comune.fi.it), at Piazza delle Murate in the Sant'Ambrogio district, is now a cultural centre, with two large halls and several smaller exhibition spaces. Box Office, the main outlet for concert and theatre tickets, has its main branch here, and there's a nice café as well. It's open daily from noon to midnight.

Oltrarno

The artisanal quarter of the city, the Oltrarno – literally "beyond the Arno" – contains several of the city's key sights. The biggest of these, Palazzo Pitti, is a colossal palace whose cluster of museums includes the city's second-ranking picture gallery, and whose garden, the Giardino di Bóboli, is Italy's most visited. Close by, the main church of Oltrarno, Santo Spirito, overlooks a piazza that typifies the gentrification that's happening in some parts of this quarter. From Santo Spirito it's a brief stroll to Santa Maria del Carmine, where the Cappella Brancacci contains an epoch-defining fresco cycle. On the other side of Oltrarno, the medieval Via dei Bardi and its continuation, Via San Niccolò, take you past the engagingly eclectic Museo Bardini, which you can visit en route to the Romanesque gem of San Miniato al Monte. Other major sights include Santa Felìcita and the extraordinary waxworks of La Specola. And on top of all this, there's a greater concentration of good bars and restaurants here than in any other part of Florence – indeed, so popular has the Piazza Santo Spirito area become with tourists that it's known to some locals as "Santo Spiritoland", just as the equivalent on the other side of the river has been dubbed "Santa Croceland".

The Ponte Vecchio at sunrise

The Ponte Vecchio

MAP p.102, POCKET MAP B13

The direct route from the city centre to the heart of the Oltrarno crosses the Arno via the Ponte Vecchio, the "old bridge". Until 1218 the crossing here was the city's only bridge, though the version you see today dates from 1345, built to replace a wooden bridge swept away by floods twelve years earlier. The Ponte Vecchio has always been loaded with shops like those now propped over the water. Their earliest tenants were butchers and fishmongers, attracted to the site by the proximity of the river, which provided a convenient dumping ground for their waste. The current plethora of jewellers dates from 1593, when Ferdinando I evicted the butchers' stalls and other practitioners of what he called "vile arts". In their place he installed eight jewellers and 41 goldsmiths, also taking the opportunity to double the rents. Florence had long revered the art of the goldsmith, and several of its major artists were skilled in the craft: Ghiberti, Donatello and Cellini, for example. The third of this trio is celebrated by a bust in the centre of the bridge.

Santa Felìcita

MAP p.102, POCKET MAP D7
Piazza Santa Felìcita. Mon–Sat 9.30am–12.30pm & 3.30–5.30pm. Free.

Some claim that Santa Felìcita has an even longer lineage than San Lorenzo (see p.70), and that a church was founded here in the second century by Greek or Syrian merchants. What's known for certain is that a church existed on this site by the fifth century, by which time it had been dedicated to St Felicity; new churches were built in the eleventh and fourteenth centuries, then in 1565 Vasari added an elaborate portico to accommodate the *corridoio* linking the Uffizi and Palazzo

Santa Felicita

Pitti; a window from the corridor looks directly into the church.

The interior demands a visit for the amazing Pontormo paintings in the **Cappella Capponi**, which lies to the right of the main door, surrounded by obstructive railings. The chapel was designed in the 1420s by Brunelleschi, but subsequently much altered – notably by Vasari, who destroyed the Pontormo fresco in the cupola when building his corridor. Under the cupola are four tondi of the Evangelists (painted with help from Pontormo's adoptive son, Bronzino), while on opposite sides of the window on the right wall are the Virgin and the angel of Pontormo's delightfully simple *Annunciation*. The low level of light admitted by this window was a determining factor in the startling colour scheme of the painter's *Deposition* (1525–28), one of the masterworks of Florentine Mannerism. Nothing in this picture is conventional: Mary is on a different scale from her attendants; the figures bearing Christ's body are androgynous beings clad in acidic sky-blue, puce green and candy-floss pink drapery; and there's no sign of the Cross, the thieves, or any of the other scene-setting devices usual in paintings of this subject.

Palazzo Pitti

MAP p.102, POCKET MAP C7–D7
Piazza Pitti ⓦ uffizi.firenze.it. Palazzo Pitti
museums open Tues–Sun 8.15am–6.50pm.
March–Oct €16, Nov–Feb €10; half-price
entrance before 9.25am; annual pass €35;
3-day pass for Palazzo Pitto museums,
Bóboli gardens & Uffizi €38/18.

Beyond Santa Felìcita, the street
opens out at Piazza Pitti, forecourt
of the largest palace in Florence,
the Palazzo Pitti. Banker and
merchant Luca Pitti commissioned
the palace in the 1450s to outdo
his rivals, the Medici, but in 1549
the cash-strapped Pitti were forced
to sell out – to the Medici. This
subsequently became the Medicis'
base in Florence, growing in bulk
until the seventeenth century,
when it achieved its present
gargantuan dimensions. Later,
during Florence's brief tenure
as the Italian capital between
1865 and 1871, it housed the
Italian kings.

Today the Palazzo Pitti and
the pavilions of the Giardino di
Bóboli contain eight museums, of
which the foremost is the **Galleria
Palatina**, an art collection second
in importance only to the Uffizi.
The Palatina possesses superb
works by Fra' Bartolomeo, Filippo
and Filippino Lippi, Caravaggio,
Rosso Fiorentino and Canova, no
fewer than seventeen pieces by
Andrea del Sarto, and numerous
paintings by **Raphael** and **Titian**.

When Raphael settled in
Florence in 1505, he was besieged
with commissions from patrons
delighted to find an artist for
whom the creative process involved
so little agonizing. Among the
masterpieces on show here are
Raphael's portraits of Angelo
Doni and his wife, Maddalena,
and the wonderful *Madonna
della Seggiola* (Madonna of the
Chair), which was once Italy's most
popular image of the Madonna –
nineteenth-century copyists had to

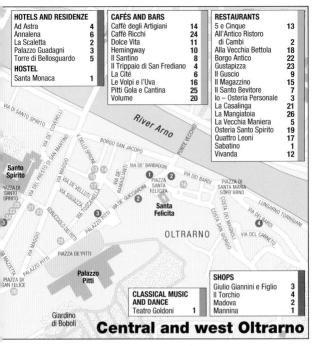

HOTELS AND RESIDENZE	
Ad Astra	4
Annalena	6
La Scaletta	2
Palazzo Guadagni	5
Torre di Bellosguardo	5
HOSTEL	
Santa Monaca	1

CAFÉS AND BARS	
Caffè degli Artigiani	14
Caffè Ricchi	24
Dolce Vita	11
Hemingway	10
Il Santino	8
Il Trippaio di San Frediano	4
La Cité	6
Le Volpi e l'Uva	16
Pitti Gola e Cantina	25
Volume	20

RESTAURANTS	
5 e Cinque	13
All'Antico Ristoro di Cambi	2
Alla Vecchia Bettola	18
Borgo Antico	22
Gustapizza	23
Il Guscio	9
Il Magazzino	15
Il Santo Bevitore	7
Io – Osteria Personale	3
La Casalinga	21
La Mangiatoia	26
La Vecchia Maniera	5
Osteria Santo Spirito	19
Quattro Leoni	17
Sabatino	1
Vivanda	12

CLASSICAL MUSIC AND DANCE	
Teatro Goldoni	1

SHOPS	
Giulio Giannini e Figlio	3
Il Torchio	4
Madova	2
Mannina	1

Central and west Oltrarno

join a five-year waiting list to study the picture. According to Vasari, the model for the famous *Donna Velata* (Veiled Woman), in the Sala di Giove, was the painter's mistress, a Roman baker's daughter known to posterity as La Fornarina.

The paintings by Titian include a number of his most trenchant portraits. The lecherous and scurrilous Pietro Aretino – journalist, critic, poet and one of Titian's closest friends – was so thrilled by his portrait that he gave it to Cosimo I. Also here are likenesses of Philip II of Spain and the young Cardinal Ippolito de' Medici, also the so-called *Portrait of an Englishman*, who scrutinizes the viewer with unflinching sea-grey eyes. To his left, by way of contrast, is the same artist's sensuous and much-copied *Mary Magdalene*, the first of a series on this theme produced for the Duke of Urbino. In the same room, look out for the gallery's outstanding sculpture, Canova's *Venus Italica*, commissioned by Napoleon as a replacement for the *Venus de' Medici*, which he had whisked off to Paris.

The Palazzo Pitti

East Oltrarno

Much of the rest of the Pitti's first floor comprises the **Appartamenti Reali**, the Pitti's state rooms; after Raphael and Titian it can be difficult to sustain a great deal of enthusiasm for such ducal elegance, notwithstanding the sumptuousness of the furnishings.

On the floor above the Palatina is the **Galleria d'Arte Moderna**, which comprises a chronological survey of primarily Tuscan art from the mid-eighteenth century to 1945. Much space is devoted to the work of the Macchiaioli (the open-air painters who were in some respects the Italian equivalent of the Impressionists), but there's a lot of mediocre stuff here, with ranks of academically proficient portraits, bombastic history paintings and sentimental dross such as Rodolfo Morgari's *Raphael Dying* and Gabriele Castagnola's depiction of Fra' Filippo Lippi on the brink of kissing the lovely young novice, Lucrezia Buti.

The **Tesoro dei Granduchi**, entered from the main palace courtyard, is a colossal museum not just of silverware but of luxury artefacts acquired by the Medici. The craftsmanship on show is astounding, even if the final products are likely to strike you as being in dubious taste – room after room is packed with seashell figurines, cups made from ostrich eggs, portraits in stone inlay, bizarre ivory carvings, and the like. Amid all the trinkets, look out for the death mask of Lorenzo il Magnifico.

Visitors without a specialist interest are unlikely to be riveted by the two remaining museums currently open. In the Palazzina della Meridiana, the eighteenth-century southern wing of the Pitti, the **Galleria del Costume** provides the opportunity to see the dress that

SHOP	
Stefano Bemer	**1**

CAFÉS AND BARS	
Fuori Porta	**4**
Il Rifrullo	**3**
Zoe	**1**

RESTAURANT	
Osteria Antica Mescita San Niccolò	**2**

Eleonora di Toledo was buried in (it's the one she's wearing in Bronzino's portrait of her in the Palazzo Vecchio). The well-presented but esoteric collection of porcelain, the **Museo delle Porcellane**, is located at the top of the Bóboli Garden.

Giardino di Bóboli

Grotta del Buontalenti

The Giardino di Bóboli

MAP p.102, POCKET MAP B9–D7
Opens daily at 8.15am; March closes
5.30pm; April, May, Sept & Oct closes
6.30pm; June–Aug closes 7.30pm; Nov–Feb
closes 4.30pm; closed 1st & last Mon of
month. March–Oct €10, Nov–Feb €6, joint
ticket with Giardino Bardini, which can be
entered from the upper part of the Bóboli.

The land occupied by the formal
gardens of the Palazzo Pitti,
the Giardino di Bóboli, was
once a quarry; the bedrock
here is one of the sources of
the yellow sandstone known
as *pietra forte* (strong stone)
that gives much of Florence its
dominant hue. When the Medici
acquired the house they set about
transforming their back yard into
an enormous garden, its every
statue, view and grotto designed
to elevate nature by the judicious
application of art. The resulting
landscape takes its name from
the **Bóboli family**, erstwhile
owners of some of the land.
Opened to the public in 1766,
this is the only really extensive
area of accessible greenery in
the centre of the city. It attracts
some five million visitors
annually, more than any other
Italian garden.

Of all the garden's Mannerist
embellishments, the most
celebrated is the **Grotta del
Buontalenti** (1583–88), to the
left of the entrance, beyond
Giambologna's much-reproduced
statue of Cosimo I's favourite
dwarf astride a giant tortoise.
Embedded in the grotto's faked
stalactites and encrustations
are replicas of Michelangelo's
Slaves – the originals were lodged
here until 1908. Lurking in the
deepest recesses of the cave, and
normally viewable only from afar,
is Giambologna's *Venus Emerging
from her Bath*, leered at by
attendant imps.

Another spectacular set-piece
is the fountain island called the
Isolotto, which is the focal point
of the far end of the garden;
from within the Bóboli the most
dramatic approach is along the
central cypress avenue known as
the **Viottolone**, many of whose
statues are Roman originals.

The Forte di Belvedere

The Forte di Belvedere, the fortress that overlooks the back of
the Pitti, was built by Buontalenti on the orders of Ferdinando I
between 1590 and 1595, ostensibly to protect the city, but in fact
to intimidate the grand duke's subjects. The urban panorama from
here is superb, but the Belvedere is open only when exhibitions
are being held in and around the shed-like palace in the centre of
the fortress.

La Specola

MAP p.102, POCKET MAP C8
Via Romana 17. June–Sept: 10.30am–5.30pm; Oct–May: 9.30am–4.30pm. €6.
On the third floor of the university buildings on Via Romana there lurks what can reasonably claim to be the strangest museum in the city. Taking its name from the telescope (*specola*) on its roof, La Specola is a twin-sectioned **museum of zoology**. The first part is conventional enough, with ranks of shells, insects and crustaceans, followed by a mortician's ark of animals stuffed, pickled and desiccated. Beyond some rather frayed-looking sharks lie the things everyone comes to see, the **Cere Anatomiche** (Anatomical Waxworks). Wax arms, legs and organs cover the walls, arrayed around satin beds on which wax cadavers recline in progressive stages of deconstruction, each muscle fibre and nerve cluster moulded and dyed with absolute precision. Most of the six hundred models were made between 1775 and 1791 by Clemente Susini, and were intended as teaching aids, in an age when medical ethics and refrigeration techniques were not what they are today.

The grisliest section of La Specola consists of a trio of tableaux that were moulded in the late seventeenth century by **Gaetano Zumbo**, a cleric from Sicily who was one of the pioneers of the art of anatomical waxwork. Whereas Susini's masterpieces were created to educate, these were made to horrify, and to horrify one man in particular: the hypochondriacal Cosimo III. Enclosed in tasteful display cabinets, they depict Florence during the plague, with rats teasing the intestines from rotting corpses, and the pink bodies of the freshly dead heaped on the suppurating semi-decomposed. A fourth tableau, illustrating the horrors of syphilis, was damaged in the 1966 flood, and now consists of a loose gathering of the deceased and diseased. Alongside is displayed a dissected waxwork head, built on the foundation of a real skull; it's as fastidious as any of Susini's creations, but Zumbo couldn't resist giving the skin a tint of putrefaction, before applying a dribble of blood to the mouth and nose.

OLTRARNO

Wax cadaver in La Specola

Santo Spirito

Santo Spirito

MAP p.102, POCKET MAP C7
Piazza Santa Spirito. Mon, Tues & Thurs–
Sat 10am–12.30pm & 4–5.30pm, Sun
4–5.30pm. Free.

Designed in 1434 as a replacement
for a thirteenth-century church,
Santo Spirito was one of
Brunelleschi's last projects, a
swansong later described by
Bernini as "the most beautiful
church in the world". Its plan
is extremely sophisticated: a
Latin cross with a continuous
chain of 38 chapels round the
outside and a line of 35 columns
running without a break
round the nave, transepts and
chancel. The exterior wall was
designed to follow the curves
of the chapels' walls; as built,
however, the exterior is plain
and straight, and the facade was
never completed. Inside, only the
Baroque baldachin disrupts the
harmony of Brunelleschi's design.

A fire in 1471 destroyed most
of Santo Spirito's medieval works,
including frescoes by Cimabue
and the Gaddi family, but as a
result the altar paintings comprise
an unusually unified collection
of religious works, the majority
having been commissioned in
the aftermath of the fire. Most
prolific among the artists is
the so-called **Maestro di Santo
Spirito**, but the finest single
painting is Filippino Lippi's
Nerli Altarpiece (c.1488), an
age-darkened Madonna and
Child with saints, which hangs
in the south transept. A door
in the north aisle leads through
to Giuliano da Sangallo's
stunning vestibule and **sacristy**
(1489–93), the latter designed
in imitation of Brunelleschi's
Cappella dei Pazzi. Hanging
above the altar is a delicate
wooden crucifix attributed to the
young Michelangelo.

The 1471 fire destroyed much
of the rest of the monastery, with
the exception of its refectory
(entered to the left of the main
church), which is now the home
of the **Fondazione Salvatore
Romano** (Mon & Sat 10am–5pm,
Sun 1–5pm; €7 joint ticket with
Cappella Brancacci), a one-
room collection comprising an
assortment of carvings, many of

them Romanesque, and a huge fresco of *The Crucifixion* (1365) by Orcagna and his workshop.

The Cappella Brancacci

MAP p.102, POCKET MAP B6
Piazza del Carmine Ⓦ museicivicifiorentini.
comune.fi.it. Mon & Wed–Sat 10am–5pm,
Sun 1–5pm. €6 or €7 on Mon, Sat & Sun
including admission to Fondazione
Savlatore Romano.

In 1771 **fire** wrecked the Carmelite convent and church of Santa Maria del Carmine some 300m west of Santo Spirito, but somehow the flames did not damage the frescoes of the church's **Cappella Brancacci**, a cycle of paintings that is one of the essential sights of Florence. The chapel is barricaded off from the rest of the Carmine, and visits are restricted to a maximum of thirty people at a time, for an inadequate fifteen minutes at peak periods.

The decoration of the chapel was begun in 1424 by **Masolino** and **Masaccio**, when the former was aged 41 and the latter just 22. Within a short time the elder was taking lessons from the younger, whose grasp of the texture of the real world, of the principles of perspective, and of the dramatic potential of the biblical texts they were illustrating far exceeded that of his precursors. In 1428 Masolino was called away to Rome, where he was followed by Masaccio a few months later. Neither would return to the chapel. Masaccio died the same year, aged just 27, but, in the words of Vasari, "All the most celebrated sculptors and painters since Masaccio's day have become excellent and illustrious by studying their art in this chapel."

The Brancacci frescoes are as startling as the Sistine Chapel in Rome, the brightness and delicacy of their colours and the solidity of the figures exemplifying what Bernard Berenson singled out as the tactile quality of Florentine art. The small scene on the left of the entrance arch is the quintessence of Masaccio's art. Depictions of **The Expulsion of Adam and Eve** had never before captured the desolation of the sinners so graphically – Adam presses his hands to his face in bottomless despair, Eve raises her head and screams. In contrast, Masolino's dainty *Adam and Eve*, opposite, pose as if to have their portraits painted.

St Peter is chief protagonist of most of the remaining scenes, some of which were left unfinished in 1428 – work did not resume until 1480, when the frescoes were completed by **Filippino Lippi**. One of the scenes finished by Lippi is the *Raising of Theophilus's Son and St Peter Enthroned*, which depicts St Peter bringing the son of the Prefect of Antioch to life and then preaching to the people of the city. The three figures to the right of his throne are thought to be Masaccio, Alberti and Brunelleschi.

The Cappella Brancacci, Santa Maria del Carmine

OLTRARNO

The Museo Stefano Bardini

MAP p.104, POCKET MAP E7
Piazza de' Mozzi 1 Ⓦ museicivicifiorentini
.comune.fi.it. Fri–Mon 11am–5pm. €6.

The Museo Stefano Bardini, which stands at the end of the handsome Via de' Bardi, houses the collection of **Stefano Bardini** (1836–1922), once the most important art dealer in Italy, whose tireless activity laid the cornerstone of many important European and American museums. Determined that no visitor to his native city should remain unaware of his success, he bought the former monastery of San Gregorio alla Pace, and converted it into a vast house for himself and his collection. Sculpture, paintings, ceramics, armour, furniture, picture frames, carpets, wooden ceilings, tombstones – Bardini bought it all, and he bequeathed the whole lot to the city. Reopened in 2011 after a protracted restoration, the museum now looks much as it did when Bardini died, though a few pieces – notably Pietro Tacca's bronze boar and Giambologna's so-called *Diavolino* (Little Devil) – were added after his death.

The Bardini is more like a colossal **showroom** than a modern museum, with miscellaneous unlabelled objets d'art strewn all about the place, often following their owner's personal logic. The most interesting items are **upstairs**, where you'll find two reliefs of the *Madonna and Child* that may be by Donatello (in a room that's stacked with similar reliefs), a beautiful terracotta *Virgin Annunciate* from fifteenth-century Siena, and some fine drawings by Giambattista Tiepolo and his son Lorenzo. Most of the paintings are unremarkable, but there are exceptions, notably Guercino's *Atlas*, Michele Giambono's *St John the Evangelist*, and a *St Michael* by Antonio del Pollaiuolo. The main staircase is hung with gorgeous carpets, the largest of which was damaged by Hitler's spurs when it was laid out to welcome the Führer at Santa Maria Novella station.

Giardino Bardini

MAP p.104, POCKET MAP E8
Entrances at Costa di San Giorgio 2 and Via de' Bardi 1r Ⓦ bardinipeyron.it. Opens daily at 8.15am; March closes 5.30pm; April, May, Sept & Oct closes 6.30pm; June–Aug closes 7.30pm; Nov–Feb closes 4.30pm; closed 1st & last Mon of month. €7 joint ticket with Tesoro dei Granduchi, Museo delle Porcellane, Galleria del Costume & Giardino di Bóboli.

The Giardino Bardini occupies the slope that was formerly the olive grove of the **Palazzo dei Mozzi**, a colossal house built in the late thirteenth century by the Mozzi family, at that time one of the richest families in Florence. (The palazzo houses a collection of seven hundred paintings donated to the city in 1937 by Fortunata Carobbi Corsi; there's a plan to put them on public show.)

After Stefano Bardini bought the property in 1913 he set about creating a semi-formal garden which has now been restored to

The Museo Stefano Bardini

Giardino Bardini

the appearance he gave it, with a neo-Baroque staircase and terraces dividing the fruit-growing section from the miniature woodland of the "*bosco inglese*". At the summit of the garden, reached by a lovely long pergola of wisteria and hortensia, a colonnaded belvedere gives a splendid view of the city.

Villa Bardini

MAP p.104, POCKET MAP E8
Costa di San Giorgio 2 Ⓦ bardinipeyron.it.
Tues–Sun 10am–7pm. €8.

At the top of the Giardino Bardini stands the Villa Bardini, built in the seventeenth century and extended by Stefano Bardini. Having been thoroughly restored, the villa is used as an exhibition space and also houses a museum dedicated to **Pietro Annigoni** (1910–88), a vehemently anti-Modernist painter who was best known for his portraits of luminaries such as Pope John XXIII and Queen Elizabeth II. Fashionistas may enjoy the villa's collection of clothes created by Roberto Capucci (born 1930). Dubbed the "Givenchy of Rome" by his admirers, Capucci made his name with frocks that seemed intent on upstaging their wearer – one of his most celebrated creations was a nine-layered dress that became famous when worn by a model in Cadillac ads in the 1950s. One-off exhibitions at the Bardini are held on the third floor, and are usually free; the third floor has another attraction – a belvedere that gives you a glorious view of the city.

The city gates and Piazzale Michelangelo

MAP p.104, POCKET MAP G8
In medieval times San Niccolò was close to the edge of the city, and two of Florence's fourteenth-century gates still stand in the vicinity: the diminutive **Porta San Miniato**, set in a portion of the walls, and the huge **Porta San Niccolò**, overlooking the Arno. From either of these gates you can begin the climb up to San Miniato: the path from Porta San Niccolò weaves up through **Piazzale Michelangelo**, with its replica *David* and fine views; the more direct path from Porta San Miniato leads to the stepped Via di San Salvatore al Monte, which emerges a short distance uphill from Piazzale Michelangelo.

San Miniato al Monte

San Miniato al Monte

MAP p.104, POCKET MAP G9
Via del Monte alle Croci. Mon–Sat
9.30am–1pm & 3–7pm, Sun 3–7pm. Free.

Perhaps the finest Romanesque structure in Tuscany, San Miniato al Monte is also the oldest sacred building in Florence after the Baptistery. The dedicatee is **St Minias**, Florence's first home-grown martyr. Legend has it that after decapitation in the centre of the city, the saintly corpse was seen to carry his severed head up the hill to this spot. A chapel devoted to Minias was built here in the eighth century, though construction of the present building began in 1013. Initially a Benedictine foundation, since 1373 it has belonged to the Olivetans, a Benedictine offshoot.

The lower part of the gorgeous marble facade is possibly eleventh-century, while the upper levels date from the twelfth century onwards, and were financed in part by the Arte di Calimala (cloth merchants' guild): their trademark, an eagle clutching a bale of cloth, perches up top.

The floor of the sublime **interior** is adorned by an elaborately patterned pavement that's dated 1207, while the middle of the nave is dominated by the lovely tabernacle designed in 1448 by Michelozzo. Steps either side of the tabernacle lead down to the **crypt**, where the original high altar contains the alleged bones of St Minias. Above, the **choir** and **presbytery** have a magnificent Romanesque pulpit and screen, and a great mosaic of *Christ Pantocrator*, created in 1297. Off the presbytery lies the **sacristy** (€1), whose walls are covered in a superlative fresco cycle by Spinello Aretino (1387), illustrating the life of St Benedict.

Back in the lower body of the church, off the left side of the nave, the **Cappella del Cardinale del Portogallo** constitutes one of Renaissance Florence's supreme examples of artistic collaboration. Completed in 1473, it was designed by Antonio di Manetto, a pupil and biographer of Brunelleschi, while the tomb was carved by Antonio and Bernardo Rossellino. The carefully integrated frescoes and paintings are by Alesso Baldovinetti, but Antonio and Piero del Pollaiuolo produced the main altarpiece (this is a copy, the original being in the Uffizi). The ceiling's tiled decoration and four glazed terracotta medallions were provided by Luca della Robbia.

Shops

Giulio Giannini e Figlio

MAP p.102, POCKET MAP C7
Piazza Pitti 36r ☏ 055 212 621,
Ⓦ giuliogiannini.it. Mon–Sat 10am–7pm,
Sun 11am–6.30pm.

Established in 1856, this paper-making and book-binding firm has been honoured with exhibitions dedicated to its work. Once the only place in Florence to make its own marbled papers, it now also offers a wide variety of diaries, address books and so forth.

Il Torchio

MAP p.102, POCKET MAP E7
Via de' Bardi 17 ☏ 055 234 2862,
Ⓦ legatoriailtorchio.com. Mon–Fri
10am–1.30pm & 2.30–7pm, Sat
10am–1pm.

Founded in 1980 and now owned by young Sicilian-Canadian Erin Ciulla, Il Torchio produces marbled paper, desk accessories, diaries, albums and other items in paper and leather.

Madova

MAP p.102, POCKET MAP D7
Via Guicciardini 1r ☏ 055 239 6526,
Ⓦ madova.com. Mon–Sat 10.30am–7pm.

The last word in gloves – every colour, every size, every style, lined with lambswool, silk, cashmere or nothing. Prices range from around €50 to €200.

Mannina

MAP p.102, POCKET MAP D7
Via Guicciardini 16r ☏ 055 282 895,
Ⓦ manninafirenze.com. Mon–Sat
9.30am–7.30pm.

This famed Oltrarno shoemaker has been going since the 1950s, when it was founded by Calogero Mannina, father of the current boss, Antonio. He produces beautifully made and sensible footwear at prices that are far from extravagant – many styles under €200 for women and €400 for men.

Stefano Bemer

MAP p.104, POCKET MAP G8
Via San Niccolò 2 ☏ 055 211 356,
Ⓦ stefanobemer.it. Mon–Sat 10am–7pm.

If you're in the market for made-to-measure Italian shoes of the very highest quality, there's no better place than this – prior to his premature death in 2012, Stefano Bemer was revered as perhaps Italy's finest shoemaker, and his apprentices continue to produce footwear to Stefano's demanding standards. The shop also sells Bemer'S [sic], the off-the-peg (but still expensive) footwear designed by Stefano and his brother Mario.

Gloves for sale in Madova

Fuori Porta

Cafés & bars

Caffè Degli Artigiani

MAP p.102, POCKET MAP D7
Via dello Sprone 16r ☎ 055 291 882.
Daily 8am–1am.

This cute little bar-café in the corner of Piazza Passera is an excellent spot for a recuperative coffee or spritz after a tour of the Pitti palace. Nice cakes too, and the menu has some interesting salads for a light lunch.

Caffè Ricchi

MAP p.102, POCKET MAP C7
Piazza di Santo Spirito 9r ☎ 055 215 864.
Summer Mon–Sat 7am–1am; winter closes 10pm; closed last 2 weeks of Feb & Aug.

In business since 1957, this is the oldest and the smartest of the café-bars on this square, with a good selection of cakes, ice cream and lunchtime snacks, and superb coffee. The owners also have a good restaurant next door.

Dolce Vita

MAP p.102, POCKET MAP B6
Piazza del Carmine ☎ 055 284 595,
ⓦ dolcevitafirenze.it. Daily 7pm–2am.

This glossy bar has been going for more than 30 years and has stayed ahead of the game by constantly updating – it reopened in 2015 after a nine-month refit, and is once again one of the coolest places in town in Oltrarno. Install yourself on the terrace or a bar stool and preen with Florence's beautiful young things. There's frequent live music (Latin, rock or jazz) and DJs on other nights, and lavish aperitivi from 7.30pm to 10pm.

Fuori Porta

MAP p.104, POCKET MAP F8
Via del Monte alle Croci 10r ☎ 055 234 2483, ⓦ fuoriporta.it. Mon–Fri 12.30–3pm & 7–11.30pm, Sat & Sun noon–11.30pm; closed two weeks mid-Aug.

If you're climbing up to San Miniato you could take a breather at this justly famous wine bar-*osteria*. There are over four hundred wines to choose from by the bottle, and an ever-changing selection by the glass, as well as a wide selection of grappas and malt whiskies. Bread, cheese, ham and salami are available, together with a choice of pasta dishes and tasty *secondi*, mainly around €10.

Hemingway

MAP p.102, POCKET MAP B6
Piazza Piattellina 9r ☎ 055 284 781. Tues–Thurs 5.30pm–1am, Fri & Sat 5pm–2am, Sun 4pm–1am.

Owners Paul de Bondt and Andrea Slitti are members of the Compagnia del Cioccolato, a chocolate appreciation society – and it shows: the chocolate desserts and handmade chocolates are sublime. You can also choose from one of countless speciality teas, sample over twenty coffees, or knock back one of the "tea cocktails".

Il Rifrullo

MAP p.104, POCKET MAP F8
Via San Niccolò 53–57r ☎ 055 234 2621,
Ⓦ ilrifrullo.com. Daily 8am–1am; closed
2 weeks in Aug.

Lying to the east of the Ponte
Vecchio–Pitti Palace route, this
place attracts fewer tourists
than many Oltrarno café-bars.
Delicious snacks with the early-
evening *aperitivi* (when the
music≈gets turned up), as well
as more substantial (and quite
pricey) dishes in the restaurant
section. There's a pleasant garden
terrace, too.

Il Santino

MAP p.102, POCKET MAP C6
Via Santo Spirito 60r ☎ 055 230 2820.
Daily 12.30am–11pm.

This small gastronomic
alimentari-cum-wine bar is an
offshoot of the neighbouring *Il
Santo Bevitore* (see p.117), and
is proving just as successful. The
wines on offer are top quality, as
are the snacks.

Il Trippaio di San Frediano

MAP p.102, POCKET MAP A6
Piazza dei Nerli. Mon–Fri 10am–6pm.

A bun filled with tripe or with
lampredotto (de luxe tripe),
slathered in spicy sauce, is the
quintessential Florentine snack.
If you want to give it a try, this
stall is the place. For the less
adventurous there are burgers
and hot dogs. Similar stalls
can be found by the Mercato
Nuovo, in Piazza dei Cimatori
(just to the north of Piazza della
Signora), and near to *Cibrèo*, in
Via dei Macci.

La Cité

MAP p.102, POCKET MAP B6
Borgo San Frediano 20r ☎ 055 210 387,
Ⓦ lacitelibreria.info. Mon–Sat 9am–2am,
Sun 3pm–2am.

With its huge windows,
mezzanine balcony and shelves of
books (to buy or just to browse),
this café-bar-bookshop has an
arty, quasi-Parisian ambience.
An area is set aside for live
performances (usually music).

Le Volpi e L'Uva

MAP p.102, POCKET MAP D7
Piazza dei Rossi 1r ☎ 055 239 8132,
Ⓦ levolpieluva.com. Mon–Sat 11am–9pm.

This discreet, friendly little
enoteca does good business by
concentrating on the wines of
small producers and providing
tasty cold meats and snacks to
accompany them (the selection
of cheeses is tremendous). At any
one time you can choose from at
least two dozen different wines by
the glass. In summer the shady
terrace is a very pleasant refuge
from the heat.

Pitti Gola e Cantina

MAP p.102, POCKET MAP C7
Piazza Pitti 16 ☎ 055 212 704,
Ⓦ pittigolaecantina.com. Mon & Wed–Sun
1pm–midnight; closed 2 weeks in
mid-Aug.

Small and friendly wine bar, run
by knowledgeable people; the
food – mainly cold meats and
handmade pasta – is good.

Volume

Volume

MAP p.102, POCKET MAP C7
Piazza Santo Spirito 5r ☎ 055 2381 460,
🆆 volumefirenze.com. Daily 8.30am–1am.

This is the most idiosyncratic of the bar-cafés on Piazza Santo Spirito – it used to be a workshop used by makers of hat forms, and the walls of the front room are still hung with the tools of the trade. Art works and craft items are on display in the cosy back room, along with books (*Volume* markets itself as "il caffè culturale"), and there's often live music in the evening – otherwise, expect a DJ. The atmosphere is hip and relaxed, and it's invariably busy, as are its neighbours, *Cabiria* and *Popcafé*.

Zoe

MAP p.104, POCKET MAP F7
Via dei Renai 13 ☎ 055 243 111,
🆆 zoebar.it. Daily 8.30am–3am.

Like the neighbouring *Negroni* (which is currently closed for a rebuild, having been acquired by new owners), *Zoe* is perennially popular for summer evening drinks, but also attracts lots of young Florentines right through the day. Breakfast is served from 8am–noon, lunch from noon–4pm, then it's "Aperitif" from 5–10pm (the Crimson Zoe cocktail is notorious) before the DJ gets the partying started. It also does good snacks and simple meals, and it's something of an art venue too.

Restaurants

5 e Cinque

MAP p.102, POCKET MAP C7
Piazza della Passera 1 ☎ 055 274 1585.
Tues–Sun noon–3pm & 7.30–10pm.

This busy little café-restaurant is one of the city's rare havens for vegetarians, as dishes made from organic vegetables are the focus – the wines are organic too. It's more a place for a quick and light meal than a lingering evening, but the food is good and the staff very warm. No credit cards.

All'Antico Ristoro di Cambi

MAP p.102, POCKET MAP A6
Via Sant'Onofrio 1r ☎ 055 217 134,
🆆 anticoristorodicambi.it. Mon–Sat
12.30–2.30pm & 7–10.30pm.

Run by the same family since the 1940s, this big, efficient yet homely trattoria is particularly good for meaty Florentine standards such as wild boar and steak, and has a fine wine list. It's vast, but nonetheless gets packed on a Saturday night, when even the large terrace fills up with a mixture of locals and visitors. Main dishes from around €15.

Alla Vecchia Bettola

MAP p.102, POCKET MAP A7
Viale Vasco Pratolini 3–7 ☎ 055 224 158,
🆆 florence.ala.it/bettola. Tues–Sat
noon–2.30pm & 7.30–10.30pm.

Located on a major traffic intersection a couple of minutes' walk from the Carmine, this wonderfully old-fashioned place – with its marble-topped

Borgo Antico

tables – has something of the atmosphere of an old-style drinking den, which is what it once was; it boasts a good repertoire of Tuscan meat dishes, with main courses mostly €12–15. No credit cards.

Borgo Antico

MAP p.102, POCKET MAP C7
Piazza di Santo Spirito 6r ⊙ 055 210 437, ⓦ borgoanticofirenze.com. Daily noon–midnight.

With its smartly unfussy decor of white tiles and ochre plasterwork, the *Borgo Antico* reflects the increasingly trendy character of this once notoriously sleazy Oltrarno piazza. In summer the outside tables here are invariably packed, and the majority of the clientele are usually foreigners. But *Borgo Antico* is not one of Florence's cynical tourist-traps: the food (pizza plus Tuscan standards) is generally good, prices are fair, and the servings are generous to a fault.

Gustapizza

MAP p.102, POCKET MAP C7
Via Maggio 46r. Tues–Sun 11.30am–3pm & 7–11pm.

The wood-fired Neapolitan pizzas served here are the best in Oltrarno – and pizzas are all they do, which is always a good thing. It's cheap, busy and basic, and no reservations are taken, so be prepared to queue.

Il Guscio

MAP p.102, POCKET MAP A6
Via dell'Orto 49 ⊙ 055 224 421, ⓦ ristorante-ilguscio.it. Mon–Fri 12.30–2pm & 7.30–11pm, Sat 7.30–11pm only; closed Aug.

This smart rustic-style restaurant is a long-established Oltrano favourite: high-quality Tuscan meat and fish dishes, superb desserts and a wide-ranging wine list. And it's not terribly pricey – you'll pay in the region of €40 per person.

Gustapizza

Il Magazzino

MAP p.102, POCKET MAP C7
Piazza della Passera 2–3 ⊙ 055 215 969. Daily noon–3pm & 7.30–11pm.

Occupying a corner of the very lively little Piazza Passera, *Il Magazzino* is an earthily authentic but high-class *osteria-tripperia*, serving hearty dishes of pasta, tripe and beef at around €10–18.

Il Santo Bevitore

MAP p.102, POCKET MAP C6
Via Santo Spirito 64–66r ⊙ 055 211 264, ⓦ ilsantobevitore.com. Mon–Sat 12.30–2.30pm & 7.30–11pm, Sun 7.30–11pm.

"The Holy Drinker" is an airy, stylish and hugely popular gastronomic *enoteca* with a small but classy menu of seasonal food (around €15–20 for a *secondi*) to complement its enticing wine list. Very busy throughout the year, especially in the evenings, so you'd best book a table. The platters of cold meats and cheese make an excellent lunch.

La Casalinga

IO – Osteria Personale

MAP p.102, POCKET MAP A6
Borgo San Frediano 167r ☎ 055 933 1341,
🌐 io-osteriapersonale.it. Mon–Sat
7.30–10pm.

Run by a young and imaginative
team, this is one of the very best
restaurants to have opened in
Florence in recent years. The
minimalist decor – bare brick
walls and very upright chairs –
send out the message that this
place is serious about its food,
and not just another purveyor of
routine Tuscan recipes. There are
no antipasti or pasta courses here,
and no *bistecca* – what you get
instead is an inventive and concise
array of seafood and meat dishes
(main courses around €20), with
the option of selecting your own
tasting menus at €40, €48 or €55.
Ingredients are seasonal and local
(the suppliers are listed on the
menu) and the wines come from
small vineyards, as you might
expect from a restaurant that is
underpinned by personal values.

La Casalinga

MAP p.102, POCKET MAP C7
Via del Michelozzo 9r ☎ 055 218 624,
🌐 trattorialacasalinga.it. Mon–Sat
noon–2.30pm & 7–10pm; closed last
3 weeks of Aug.

Located in a side street off
Piazza di Santo Spirito, this
long-established family-run
trattoria serves up some of the
best low-cost Tuscan dishes in
town. No frills – paper tablecloths,
house wine by the flask and brisk
service – but most nights it's filled
with regulars and some tourists,
and if you turn up after 8pm
without a reservation you'll almost
certainly have to queue.

La Mangiatoia

MAP p.102, POCKET MAP C7
Piazza San Felice 8–9r ☎ 055 224 060.
Tues–Sun noon–3pm & 7–10pm.

Ideally placed for lunch before or
after a visit to Palazzo Pitti, this
rosticceria–pizzeria has a very
basic trattoria out back, where
a full menu of Tuscan fare is
served in a bright and somewhat
spartan interior, with most
secondi less than €10. The pizzas,
cooked in a wood-fired oven, are
very good too.

La Vecchia Maniera

MAP p.102–107, POCKET MAP B6
Borgo San Frediano 49r ☎ 055 264 5499.
Mon & Wed–Sun noon–3pm & 7–10pm.

A small and homely trattoria,
serving classic Tuscan peasant
fare (tripe, wild boar, mixed
grills) at low prices – main
courses €10–12. Unlike many
Oltrarno restaurants, its clientele
is predominantly local, so far.

Osteria Antica Mescita
San Niccolò

MAP p.104, POCKET MAP F8
Via San Niccolò 60r ☎ 055 234 2836,
🌐 osteriasanniccolo.it. Daily noon–
midnight; closed Aug.

This genuine old-style *osteria*
has a small menu of robust and
well-prepared Florentine staples
(*ribollita*, *lampredotto*, etc), at
around €10–15 for main courses.
The downstairs dining room is an
atmospheric spot – it was formerly
a crypt of the adjacent church of
San Niccolò.

Osteria Santo Spirito

MAP p.102, POCKET MAP C7
Piazza di Santo Spirito 16r ☎ 055 238
2383, Ⓦ osteriasantospirito.it. Daily
11am–11pm.

Run by the owners of the *Borgo Antico* (see p.117), this modern *osteria* is likewise a place that aims to please the tourists yet does so without sacrificing its integrity. The menu is full of the usual Tuscan meat and fish dishes, but with a touch of contemporary flair – and the portions are substantial. Tables are on two floors, and in summer you can eat outdoors on the piazza. Main courses €15–28.

Quattro Leoni

MAP p.102, POCKET MAP C7
Via dei Vellutini 1r/Piazza della Passera
☎ 055 218 562, Ⓦ 4leoni.com. Daily
noon–midnight.

One of the most pleasant places to eat in Florence: inside, there are three rooms with splashy modern paintings hung on the rough stone walls; outside, the tables are shaded by vast canvas umbrellas in a corner of the tiny Piazza della Passera. Some say the quality of the food and service has declined with its rising popularity, but it's generally a cut above the average, and the youthful vibe is refreshing. Expect to pay around €15 for a main course.

Sabatino

MAP p.102, POCKET MAP A5
Via Pisani 2r ☎ 055 225 955, Ⓦ trattoria
sabatino.it. Mon–Fri noon–2.30pm &
7.15pm–10pm; closed Aug.

The cooking at *Sabatino* is as plain as can be, as is the place itself – there's one refectory-like dining room, with big tables covered with laminated chequered cloth. But this old-fashioned family *osteria* is absolutely authentic, and it's ridiculously inexpensive. Italian cities used to have plenty of family-run no-nonsense *osterie* like this; in Florence, *Sabatino* is now one of a kind.

Vivanda

MAP p.102, POCKET MAP B6
Via Santa Monaca 7r ☎ 055 238 1208,
Ⓦ vivandafirenze.it. Daily 11am–3pm &
6pm–midnight.

Florence's first organic *enoteca* is also a small self-service restaurant, offering meals that use vegetables and oil from *Vivanda*'s own farm. Cold cuts (€15) make up the bulk of the main course menu, but there's a good choice of vegetarian pasta dishes, soups and salads.

Classical music & dance

Teatro Goldoni

MAP p.102, POCKET MAP B8
Via Santa Maria 15 ☎ 055 210 804.

This exquisite little theatre, inaugurated in 1817 and seating just 363 people, is used for chamber music, opera and dance performances.

Teatro Goldoni

OLTRARNO

The city outskirts

Two of the attractions covered in this section – the Museo Stibbert and Florence's football ground – are a stiff walk from the centre of town, but can be reached easily by public transport; the Cascine park is a stroll west from the Ognissanti district.

The Cascine

MAP p.121, POCKET MAP A4
Bus #1, 9, 12, 17 or 17c from the station, or tram.

Florence's **public park**, the Cascine, begins close to the Ponte della Vittoria, a half-hour walk west of the Ponte Vecchio, and dwindles away 3km downstream, at the confluence of the Arno and the Mugnone rivers. Once a dairy farm (*cascina*), then a hunting reserve, this narrow strip of greenery mutated into a high-society venue in the eighteenth century: Florence's *beau monde* used to relax with a promenade under the trees of the Cascine. A fountain in the park bears a dedication to Shelley, who was inspired to write his *Ode to the West Wind* while strolling here on a blustery day in 1819.

Thousands of people come out here on Tuesday mornings for the colossal **market**, and on any day of the week the Cascine swarms with joggers, cyclists and roller-bladers. Parts of the park have become markedly gentrified of late, with the closure of the huge clubs that for years were a fixture of Florence's nightlife scene, and the opening in 2014 of the Opera di Firenze concert hall at the entrance, next to the Stazione Leopolda exhibition space.

Strolling through the Cascine

City outskirts

HOSTEL	
Villa Camerata	1

MARKET	
Cascine market	1

CLUB AND VENUE	
Opera di Firenze	2
Tenax	1

The Museo Stibbert

MAP p.121, POCKET MAP E1
Via Stibbert 26 ⓦ museostibbert.it. Mon–
Wed 10am–1pm, Fri–Sun 10am–5pm.
One-hour guided tour, on the hour €8. Bus
#4 from the station.

About 1500m north of San Marco
stands the Museo Stibbert. This
rambling, murky mansion was the
home of the half-Scottish-half-
Italian Frederick Stibbert, who
in his twenties made a name for
himself in Garibaldi's army. Later
he inherited a fourteenth-century
house from his mother, then
bought the neighbouring mansion
and joined the two together, thus
creating a place big enough to
accommodate the fruits of his
compulsive collecting. The 64
rooms contain over fifty thousand
items, ranging from snuffboxes to
paintings by Carlo Crivelli and a
possible Botticelli.

Militaria were Frederick's chief
enthusiasm, and the Stibbert
armour collection is reckoned
one of the world's best. It includes
Roman, Etruscan and Japanese
examples (the highlight of the
whole museum), as well as a
fifteenth-century *condottiere*'s
outfit and the armour worn by
the great Medici soldier Giovanni
delle Bande Nere, retrieved from
his grave in San Lorenzo in 1857.
The big production number
comes in the great hall, between
the two houses, where a platoon
of mannequins is clad in full
sixteenth-century gear.

The Museo Stibbert

Stadio Artemio Franchi

MAP p.121, POCKET MAP H3
Viale Manfredo Fanti ⓦ violachannel.tv.
Bus #17 or train to Campo di Marte.

As befits this monument-stuffed city, Florence's football team play in a **stadium** that's listed as a building of cultural significance, the Stadio Artemio Franchi (or Stadio Comunale) at Campo di Marte. It was designed by Pier Luigi Nervi in 1930, and was the first major sports venue to exploit the shape-making potential of reinforced concrete – its spiral ramps, cantilevered roof and slim central tower still make quite an impact.

Following bankruptcy in 2002, Florence's football team – AC Fiorentina (ⓦ en.violachannel.tv) – was kicked out of Serie A and demoted to Serie C2B, the bottom of the heap. Most of its star players jumped ship, but the club fought its way back up the leagues, returning to Serie A for the 2004/2005 season. AC Fiorentina (known as The Viola, after their violet shirts) are now once again a securely top-flight outfit. Tickets cost from around €20 and can be bought at the ground itself or from numerous outlets in the city, the chief of which are Box Office (see p.7) and the kiosk in Via Anselmi, off Piazza della Repubblica; other points of sale are listed on the club website.

San Salvi

MAP p.121, POCKET MAP H5
Via San Salvi 16. Tues–Sun 8.15am–1.50pm.
Free. Bus #6 from the train station or Piazza San Marco, or #10 from Piazza San Marco.

Twenty minutes' walk beyond Piazza Beccaria, east of Sant'Ambrogio, is the ex-convent of San Salvi, where the most precious possession is a glorious *Last Supper* by Andrea del Sarto. As a prelude to this picture, there's a gallery of fairly unremarkable Renaissance art, and some beautiful reliefs from the tomb of Giovanni Gualberto, founder of the Vallombrosan order to which this monastery belonged. The tomb was smashed up by Charles V's troops in 1530 but they refused to damage the *Last Supper*, which is still in the refectory for which it was painted, accompanied by a pair of del Sarto frescoes brought here from other churches in Florence.

Stadio Artemio Franchi

Market

Cascine market

MAP p.121, POCKET MAP A4
Tuesday 8am–2pm.

The biggest of all Florence's markets takes place on Tuesday mornings at the Cascine park, near the banks of the Arno, where hundreds of stallholders set up an alfresco budget-class department store. Clothes (some secondhand) and shoes are the best bargains.

Club & venue

Opera di Firenze

MAP p.121, POCKET MAP A4
Viale Fratelli Rosselli 1 🕿 **055 277 9350,** 🌐 **operadifirenze.it.**

The city's hi-tech new concert hall is the centrepiece of the "Parco della Musica", a cultural zone that's being developed on the edge of the Cascine park. For operas and other big events there's a 1800-seat auditorium, complemented by a 1100-seater for recitals and a terrace for open-air performances on the roof. The TI tram from Santa Maria Novella stops right outside the venue.

Tenax

MAP p.121, POCKET MAP A3
Via Pratese 46 🕿 **055 282 340,** 🌐 **tenax .org. Fri–Sat 10pm–4am; closed mid-May to mid-Sept.**

Florence's top-ranking club, the warehouse-styled *Tenax* hosts big-name DJs. As it's located northwest, near the airport (take a taxi), you'll escape the *internazionalisti* who tend to pack the central clubs. With two large floors, it's a venue for concerts as well. In summer, when the club is shut, *Tenax* often holds one-off events at the Stazione Leopoldina, the disused train station by the new opera house. Admission from around €20.

Fashion factory outlets

Tuscany is the powerhouse of the country's textile industry, and several retail outlets within easy reach of Florence sell each season's leftovers at discounts as high as seventy percent.

Barberino Designer Outlet Via Meucci, Barberino di Mugello 🕿 055 842 161, 🌐 mcarthurglen.it/barberino. This is Barberino's biggest outlet, with some 200 brands on sale, including Furla, Guess, Michael Kors and Trussardi. Busitalia from Via Santa Caterina da Siena or shuttle bus from outside Santa Maria Novella station (2 daily). Daily 10am–8pm (till 9pm June–Aug).

Dolce & Gabbana Via Pian dell'Isola 49, Località Santa Maria Maddalena 🕿 055 833 1300. This two-storey shed is packed with clothes, accessories and household items from Dolce & Gabbana. Train to Rignano sull'Arno-Reggello, then a taxi. Mon–Sat 9am–7pm, Sun 10am–7pm.

The Mall Via Europa 8, Leccio Regello 🕿 055 865 7775, 🌐 themall .it. The Mall has outlets for Cavalli, Ferragamo and Bottega Veneta, among others, but Gucci dominates. Busitalia from Via Santa Caterina da Siena or shuttle bus from Santa Maria Novella station (3 daily). Daily 10am–7pm (till 8pm June–Aug).

Space Montevarchi 🕿 055 91 901. Stacked with Prada clothes, and a good selection from the Miu Miu diffusion label. Train to Montevarchi, then a taxi. Sun–Fri 10.30am–7.30pm, Sat 9.30am–7.30pm.

Fiesole

The hill-town of Fiesole, which spreads over a cluster of hills above the Mugnone and Arno valleys some 8km northeast of Florence, is conventionally described as a pleasant retreat from the crowds and heat of summertime Florence. Unfortunately, its tranquillity has been so well advertised that in high season it's now hardly less busy than Florence itself; that said, Fiesole offers a grandstand view of the city, has something of the feel of a country village, and bears many traces of its long history. First settled in the Bronze Age, later by the Etruscans and then absorbed by the Romans, it rivalled its neighbour until the early twelfth century, when the Florentines overran the town. From that time it became a satellite, favoured as a semi-rural second home for wealthier citizens such as the ubiquitous Medici.

The #7 ATAF bus runs every twenty minutes from Via La Pira (near the junction with Piazza San Marco) to Fiesole's central Piazza Mino da Fiesole; the journey takes around twenty minutes.

The Duomo

MAP p.124
Daily 7.30am–noon & 3–6pm; winter closes 5pm. Free.

When the Florentines wrecked Fiesole in 1125, the only major building they spared was the Duomo, on the edge

Fiesole

N

Giardini Pubblici
VIA D. MURA ETRUSCHE
San Francesco
Teatro Romano
Museo Archeologico
Sant'Alessandro
San Jacopo
Museo Bandini
PIAZZA DEL MERCATO
VIA MARINI
Duomo
PIAZZA MINO DA FIESOLE
PIAZZA GARIBALDI
VIA GRAMSCI
VIA VECCHIA FIESOLANA
VIA VERDI
VIA VECCHIA FIESOLANA
VIA FRA GIOVANNI ANGELICO
VI A MONTECECERI
VIA BADIA D. ROCCETTINI
Badia Fiesolana
VIA GIUSEPPE MANTELLINI

0 metres 200
0 yards 200

San Domenico

ACCOMMODATION
Camping Panoramico 1

RESTAURANTS
La Reggia degli Etruschi 1
Terrazza 45 2

The Duomo, Piazza Mino

of Piazza Mino. Subsequently, nineteenth-century restorers managed to ruin the exterior, which is now notable only for its lofty campanile. The most interesting part of the bare interior is the raised choir: the altarpiece is a polyptych, painted in the 1440s by Bicci di Lorenzo, and the Cappella Salutati, to the right, contains two fine pieces carved around the same time by Mino da Fiesole – an altar frontal of *The Madonna and Saints* and the tomb of Bishop Salutati. Fiesole's patron saint, St Romulus, is buried underneath the choir in the ancient crypt.

The Museo Bandini

MAP p.124
Via Dupré 1 Ⓦ museidifiesole.it. Fri–Sun: April–Sept 10am–7pm; March & Oct 10am–6pm; Nov–Feb 10am–3pm. €5, or €12 three-day ticket for all Fiesole's museums.

The Museo Bandini possesses a workaday collection of glazed terracotta in the style of the della Robbias, the odd piece of Byzantine ivory work and a few thirteenth- and fourteenth-century Tuscan pictures, none of them especially outstanding.

Teatro Romano and the Museo Archeologico

MAP p.124
Via Portigiani 1 Ⓦ museidifiesole.it. April–Sept daily 9am–7pm; March & Oct daily 10am–6pm; Nov–Feb Wed–Mon 10am–3pm. €7 for Teatro Romano, €10 for Teatro and museum, or three-day ticket for all Fiesole's museums €12.

Built in the first century BC, the three-thousand-seat Teatro Romano was excavated towards the end of the nineteenth century and is in such good repair that it's used for performances during the Estate Fiesolana festival (see p.145). Most of the exhibits in the site's small museum were excavated in this area, and encompass pieces from the Bronze Age to the Roman occupation.

San Jacopo

MAP p.124
Via San Francesco. Summer Sat & Sun 10am–7pm; winter closes 5pm. Free.

From the piazza, the steep Via San Francesco runs past the **Oratorio di San Jacopo**, a little chapel containing a fifteenth-century fresco of *The Coronation of the Virgin* and some fine examples of ecclesiastical goldsmithing. A little further up, on the left, a terrace in front of the town's war memorials offers a knockout **view** of Florence.

Sant'Alessandro

MAP p.124
Via San Francesco. Free.

The church of Sant'Alessandro, at the top of Via San Francesco, was founded in the sixth century on the site of Etruscan and Roman temples; repairs have rendered the outside a whitewashed nonentity, but the beautiful *marmorino cipollino* (onion marble) columns of the basilical interior make it the most atmospheric building in Fiesole. The bases and Ionic capitals of the columns were recycled from Roman structures. From time to time the church is used as an exhibition space; otherwise, it's very rarely open.

San Francesco

MAP p.124
Via San Francesco. Daily: April–Sept 9am–noon & 3–7pm; Oct–March 9am–noon & 3–6pm. Free.

San Francesco Church

The site of Fiesole's Etruscan acropolis is occupied by the fourteenth-century monastery of San Francesco. Its tranquil little church – which was rebuilt in neo-Gothic style in the first decade of the twentieth century – contains an *Immaculate Conception* by Piero di Cosimo (second altar on the right), and has a fine main altarpiece by Neri di Bicci. In the monastery's tiny **museum** (free) you can see a miscellany of mostly unlabelled material, much of it gathered in the course of missions to the Far East; alongside the Ming and Qing vases, there's a small array of stuff from ancient Egypt. To the right of the church is a tiny and bucolic cloister, which usually can be admired only through the gate.

From the front of San Francesco a gate opens into the wooded Giardino Pubblico, the most pleasant descent back to Piazza Mino; on the way down, you'll get a good view of the Roman ruins.

San Domenico

MAP p.124
Piazza San Domenico. Summer 7.30am–12.30pm & 4.30–6.30pm; winter 8.30am–noon & 4–6pm. Free.

The most enjoyable excursion from Fiesole is a wander down the narrow Via Vecchia Fiesolana, which passes the **Villa Medici** – built for Cosimo il Vecchio by Michelozzo – on its way to the hamlet of San Domenico. Fra' Angelico entered the Dominican order at the monastery of San Domenico, and the church retains a *Madonna and Angels* by him – it was painted for the high altar but is now in the first chapel on the left. The adjacent chapterhouse also has a Fra' Angelico fresco of *The Crucifixion* and a *Madonna and Child* that's been attributed to him; for admission, ring at no. 4, to the right of the church. The

Via San Francesco

bus back to Florence stops at San Domenico, so you don't have to trudge back up to Piazza Mino to catch it.

The Badìa Fiesolana

MAP p.124
Via dei Roccettini. Mon–Fri 9am–5.30pm, Sat 9am–noon. Free.

Five minutes' walk northwest from San Domenico stands the Badìa Fiesolana, Fiesole's **cathedral** from the ninth century to the beginning of the eleventh. Tradition has it that the building stands on the spot on which St Romulus was martyred during the reign of Domitian. Cosimo il Vecchio had the church altered in the 1460s, a project which left the magnificent Romanesque facade embedded in the rough stone frontage while the interior was transformed into a superb Renaissance building – the design is based on one drawn up by Brunelleschi. The monastic complex is now home to the European University Institute, an elite postgraduate research unit.

Restaurants

La Reggia degli Etruschi

MAP p.124
Via San Francesco 18 ☎ 055 59 385, ⓦ lareggiadeglietruschi.com. Daily 12.30–3pm & 7–10pm.

As you'd expect, Fiesole has a few restaurants to cater for the day-trippers from Florence, but none is better than this place – the food is fine (main courses around €15–20), but what makes the place really memorable is the view from its dining rooms and terraces.

Terrazza 45

MAP p.124
Piazza Mino da Fiesole 45 ☎ 055 597 259, ⓦ terrazza45.it. Tues–Sun noon–2.30 & 7–11pm.

Run by a young and very hospitable team, *Terrazza 45* is a relative newcomer to Fiesole, but it has quickly established an excellent reputation. You can eat in the stylishly monochrome dining-room or, in summer, on the panoramic terrace. Emphasis is inevitably on meat (try the pasta with wild boar), but with a few surprises, such as fried *baccalà*. Main courses around €15.

ACCOMMODATION

Palazzo Guadagni

Hotels and residenze

Demand for accommodation in Florence is almost limitless, which means that prices are high and some hoteliers less than scrupulous. There's rarely a let-up in the tourist invasion: "low season" is officially the period from mid-November to mid-March (except for Christmas and New Year), plus the weeks from mid-July to the end of August, but any time between March and October you should book your room well in advance. The tourist office opposite the train station can find you a hotel (for a fee), but you'd be ill-advised to roll into town without having somewhere already sorted out. If none of our recommended places has a room, search the listings on the official tourism website Ⓦ firenzeturismo.it. Never respond to the touts who hang around the train station: their hotels are likely to be expensive, or remote, or unlicensed private houses. Hotel prices in Florence are higher than anywhere else in Tuscany, but many places reduce their rates considerably in low season – and with the recession, online special discounts are becoming commonplace even in summer. The prices we've given are the quoted rates for a standard double in high season; bear in mind that many hotels require a two-night-minimum booking in summer.

Piazza del Duomo and around

BAVARIA MAP p.28, POCKET MAP D11. Borgo degli Albizi 26 ☎ 055 234 0313, Ⓦ hotelbavariafirenze.it. A simple and friendly one-star near the city centre, occupying part of a sixteenth-century palazzo. Has just nine rooms, including some palatial chambers on the upper floor, and several inexpensive rooms with shared bathroom. Be sure to book, as it's popular with student tour groups. **€80**

BENIVIENI MAP p.28, POCKET MAP C11. Via delle Oche 5 ☎ 055 238 2133, Ⓦ hotelbenivieni.it. This small, family-run three-star is situated between the Duomo and Piazza della Signoria, tucked away on a quiet backstreet. Fifteen rooms are ranged around two floors of a former synagogue; the rooms on the upper floor are brighter but all are simple, modern and in perfect condition. **€170**

BRUNELLESCHI MAP p.28, POCKET MAP C11. Piazza Santa Elisabetta 3 ☎ 055 27 370, Ⓦ brunelleschihotelflorence.com. Designed by architect Italo Gamberini, this four-star hotel is built around a Byzantine chapel and fifth-century tower – the city's oldest building. A small in-house museum displays Roman and other fragments found during building work. Decor is simple and stylishly modern, with earthen tones predominant; the 96 rooms and suites are spacious – the best, on the fourth floor, have views of the Duomo and Campanile. **€440**

HELVETIA & BRISTOL MAP p.28, POCKET MAP B11. Via dei Pescioni 2 ☎ 055 26 651, Ⓦ hotelhelvetiabristol.com. In business since 1894 and favoured by such luminaries as Pirandello, Stravinsky and Gary Cooper, this is undoubtedly Florence's finest small

Our top hotels and residenze

For a damn-the-cost weekend: *Helvetia & Bristol* p.130
For a romantic break: *Morandi alla Crocetta* p.134
For a room with a view: *La Scaletta* p.140
For luxury on a budget: *Antica Dimora Firenze* p.133
For a touch of history: *Brunelleschi* p.130 or *Loggiato dei Serviti* p.134
The best in Oltrarno: *Palazzo Guadagni* p.136
If you're really watching the pennies: *Cestelli* p.132

five-star hotel. The public spaces and 67 bedrooms and suites (each unique) are faultlessly designed and fitted, mixing antique furnishings and modern facilities – such as jacuzzis in many bathrooms – to create a style that evokes the *belle époque* without being twee. If you're going to treat yourself, this is a leading contender. **€320**

IL SALOTTO DI FIRENZE MAP p.28, POCKET MAP C10. Via Roma 6 ☎ 055 218 347, W ilsalottodifirenze.it. This *residenza* has six well-appointed rooms, with three overlooking Piazza del Duomo. Perhaps not a good choice if you're a light sleeper, but the standard of accommodation is high and the location unbeatable. **€190**

MAXIM MAP p.28, POCKET MAP C11. Entrances at Via dei Calzaiuoli 11 (lift) and Via de' Medici 4 (stairs) ☎ 055 217 474, W hotelmaximfirenze.it. Few three-star hotels offer a better location than this friendly 26-room place just a minute from the Duomo. The clean double rooms are excellent value, and all have en-suite bathrooms; the quietest look onto a central courtyard. **€120**

NOVECENTO MAP p.28, POCKET MAP E4. Via Ricasoli 10 ☎ 055 214 138, W bbnovecentofirenze.it. The four top-floor rooms of this very welcoming B&B are not large, but all of them are en suite and the location could hardly be more central – you're just a minute's slow stroll from the Duomo. The little rooftop terrace is an added attraction. Not one for people with mobility problems, though – there's no lift. **€130**

RESIDENZA DEI PUCCI MAP p.28, POCKET MAP E4. Via dei Pucci 9 ☎ 055 281 886, W www.residenzadeipucci.com. Located very close to the Duomo, the *Residenza dei Pucci* occupies a fine nineteenth-century

townhouse, and offers six beautifully furnished and airy rooms, each of them different from all the others. **€120**

SAVOY MAP p.28, POCKET MAP C11. Piazza della Repubblica 7 ☎ 055 27 351, W grandluxuryhotels.com. Fitted out in discreetly luxurious modern style, with plenty of bare wood, stone-coloured fabrics and peat-coloured marble, the *Savoy* is one of the city's very best hotels. Some might find it a bit too business-like, but the efficiency of the operation is impressive. And the location could not be better. **€600**

Piazza della Signoria and around

HERMITAGE MAP p.38, POCKET MAP B13. Vicolo Marzio 1/Piazza del Pesce ☎ 055 287 216, W hermitagehotel.com. Pre-booking is recommended year-round to secure one of the 28 rooms in this three-star hotel right next to the Ponte Vecchio, with unbeatable views from some rooms as well as from the flower-filled roof garden. The service is friendly, and rooms are cosy, decorated with the odd antique flourish; bathrooms are small but nicely done. **€170**

RELAIS CAVALCANTI MAP p.38, POCKET MAP B12. Via Pelliceria 2 ☎ 055 210 962, W relaiscavalcanti.com. Run by Francesca and her sister Anna, the *Relais Cavalcanti* is a homely fourth-floor guesthouse that occupies the fourth floor of a palazzo overlooking the Palazzo di Parte Guelfa and Porcellino market. The rooms are a good size and are perfectly maintained, and the location is excellent. There's a bar on the ground floor, but the glazing more than takes care of any noise. **€120**

Renting an apartment

The high cost of hotel rooms in Florence makes **self-catering** an attractive option – for the price of a week in a cramped double room in a three-star hotel you could book yourself a two-bedroom apartment right in the centre of the city. Many package-holiday companies have a few apartments in their brochures, but a trawl of the internet will throw up dozens of places at more reasonable prices. One of the best places to look is ⓦ homeaway.co.uk, a site which puts you in touch directly with the owners and features dozens of properties in Florence. Of course, the short-term rental market has been transformed in recent years by the meteoric rise of ⓦ Airbnb.com. In Florence there are now more than one thousand properties that are registered on this website, offering accommodation at prices that are often lower than even the most basic B&B. But Airbnb is not regarded as entirely a good thing in Florence. Owners of small hotels and B&Bs are unhappy at being undercut by private individuals who are not subject to the regulations by which official providers of accommodation have to abide, and there's general unease about the effect that the ever-increasing number of holiday rentals is having on accommodation costs for the people of Florence. Cities such as Barcelona and Berlin have already taken steps to limit the expansion of Airbnb; it's possible that the authorities in Florence might take action too.

RESIDENZA D'EPOCA IN PIAZZA DELLA SIGNORIA MAP p.38, POCKET MAP D12. Via dei Magazzini 2 ☏ 055 239 9546, ⓦ inpiazzadellasignoria.com. This luxurious *residenza d'epoca* has ten spacious bedrooms, several of them giving a view of the piazza. The style is antique, but tastefully restrained, and the management is very friendly. €280

West of the centre

ALESSANDRA MAP p.56, POCKET MAP B13. Borgo Santi Apostoli 17 ☏ 055 283 438, ⓦ hotelalessandra.com. An unpretentious and very good two-star, with 27 rooms (nearly all with bathroom) occupying a sixteenth-century palazzo and furnished in a mixture of antique and modern styles. Not the cheapest two-star in town, but among the most comfortable. €150

BRETAGNA MAP p.56, POCKET MAP C6. Lungarno Corsini 6 ☏ 055 289 618, ⓦ hotelbretagna.net. This three-star riverfront hotel has a superb location and Rococo-style breakfast and living rooms. Six of the 24 rooms overlook the Arno, and most of the rest have en-suite bathrooms and a/c. €180

CESTELLI MAP p.56, POCKET MAP A12. Borgo SS Apostoli 25 ☏ 055 214 213, ⓦ hotelcestelli.com. Spotlessly maintained by its young Florentine–Japanese owners, this eight-roomed one-star occupies part of a house that once belonged to a minor Medici, whose bust adorns the facade. The rooms are a good size, and most are en suite. €100

ELITE MAP p.56, POCKET MAP C4. Via della Scala 12 ☏ 055 215 395, ⓦ hotelelitefirenze.com. Of all the hotels on this street, the ten-room two-star *Elite* is the real bargain. It's basic but clean and is run by a very pleasant management. Most rooms have private bathrooms; ask for a room at the back, as Via della Scala is quite a busy road. €110

GALLERY HOTEL ART MAP p.56, POCKET MAP B13. Vicolo dell'Oro 5 ☏ 055 27 263, ⓦ lungarnohotels.com. In a small, quiet square a few paces from the Ponte Vecchio, this immensely stylish four-star is unlike any other hotel in central Florence. Owned by the Ferragamo fashion house, it has a sleek, minimalist and hyper-modern look – lots of dark wood and neutral colours – and tasteful contemporary art displayed in the reception and all 74 rooms. There's a small but smart bar, a sushi restaurant and an attractive lounge with art-filled bookshelves and comfortable sofas. **€350**

J.K. PLACE MAP p.56, POCKET MAP C5. Piazza Santa Maria Novella 7 ☎ 055 264 5181, Ⓦ jkplace.com. One of the most appealing of Florence's designer hotels occupies a fine eighteenth-century building on Piazza Santa Maria Novella. The twenty rooms of this elegant townhouse have been designed by Michele Bönan in retro-modernist hybrid style, and have DVD players and flat-screen TVs. **€560**

NIZZA MAP p.56, POCKET MAP A10. Via del Giglio 5 ☎ 055 239 6897, Ⓦ hotelnizza .com. A smart eighteen-room family-run two star, with helpful staff and very central location. All rooms are en suite, and are better furnished and decorated than many in this category. **€120**

PALAZZO DI CAMUGLIANO MAP p.56. POCKET MAP C5. Via del Moro 15 ☎ 055 265 4578, Ⓦ palazzodicamugliano.com. Occupying part of sixteenth-century mansion between Piazza Santa Maria Novella and river, this is a palatial and tranquil *residenza*, strewn with antiques and adorned with frescoes and rich stuccowork. Most of the ten rooms have a four-poster bed and beautiful wood-beam ceilings, and some of them are immense. **€320**

PORTA ROSSA MAP p.56, POCKET MAP A12. Via Porta Rossa 19 ☎ 055 271 0911, Ⓦ http://nhportarossa.hotelin firenze.com. Florence's most venerable four-star hotel, the 72-room *Porta Rossa* has been in business since the beginning of the nineteenth century and has hosted, among others, Byron and Stendhal. Recently reopened after a long renovation, it retains something of its old ambience while the rooms have been fitted out in crisp but luxuriously modern style, with red and white the dominant tones. **€250**

TORNABUONI BEACCI MAP p.56, POCKET MAP A12. Via de' Tornabuoni 3 ☎ 055 212 645, Ⓦ tornabuonihotels .com. With 28 individually decorated rooms occupying the top two floors of conjoined fifteenth-century palazzi, this antiques-stuffed four-star hotel offers the best value for money on Florence's poshest shopping street, with particularly good rates in the off-season. **€210**

TORRE GUELFA MAP p.56, POCKET MAP B12. Borgo SS Apostoli 8 ☎ 055 239 6338, Ⓦ hoteltorreguelfa.com. Twenty tastefully furnished rooms are crammed into the third floor of this ancient tower, the tallest private building in the city; there are marvellous views from the small roof garden. There are also six cheaper doubles on the first floor (no TV and more noise from the road). Though slightly shabby in places, this is a characterful hotel, and very popular. **€210**

North of the centre

ANTICA DIMORA FIRENZE MAP p.72, POCKET MAP F2. Via San Gallo 72 ☎ 055 462 7296, Ⓦ johanna.it. This plush *residenza*, run by the owners of the neighbouring *Antica Dimora Johlea* (see below), has six very comfortable double rooms, some with four-poster beds. **€110**

ANTICA DIMORA JOHLEA MAP p.72, POCKET MAP F2. Via San Gallo 80 ☎ 055 461 185, Ⓦ johanna.it. Slightly pricier and a little more luxurious than the *Antica Dimora Firenze*, this lovely *residenza* also has a nice roof terrace, giving a roofline view of the Duomo and the hills beyond. **€160**

AZZI MAP p.72, POCKET MAP D4. Via Faenza 56 ☎ 055 213 806, Ⓦ hotelazzi .com. This immensely welcoming three-star has fifteen bedrooms decorated in a cosily rustic style, with antique furnishings and garden views from most rooms. The owners are keen musicians, and sometimes put on a song recital for guests, with *aperitivi*. **€110**

CASCI MAP p.72, POCKET MAP E4. Via Cavour 13 ☎ 055 211 686, Ⓦ hotelcasci .com. It would be hard to find a more hospitable two-star in central Florence than this 26-room family-run hotel, which occupies part of a building in which Rossini once stayed. Only two (sound-proofed) rooms face the busy street; the rest are very quiet, and all are clean and neat, if somewhat compact. The welcome is unfailingly warm, the owners are immensely helpful, and the buffet breakfast – laid out under the frescoed ceiling of the reception area – is generous. **€130**

KURSAAL AUSONIA MAP p.72, POCKET MAP D3. Via Nazionale 24 ☎ 055 496 324, Ⓦ kursonia.com. Welcoming, recently refurbished three-star near the station, with accommodation ranging from spacious "superior" doubles, in faux-antique style, to rather more bland and functional "standard" rooms. **€120**

LOCANDA DEI POETI MAP p.72, POCKET MAP D3. Via Guelfa 74 ☎ 055 488 701, Ⓦ locandadeipoeti.com. Run by an actor and his partner, this small B&B has a poetry theme, as you might have guessed. Various parts of the building are dedicated to different poets, and poems are written on some of the walls. The wackiness doesn't extend to the four individually styled bedrooms, however. **€150**

LOGGIATO DEI SERVITI MAP p.72, POCKET MAP F3. Piazza Santissima Annunziata 3 ☎ 055 289 592, Ⓦ loggiatodeiservitihotel.it. Elegant three-star in one of Florence's most celebrated squares. Its 38 rooms have been incorporated into a structure designed in the sixteenth century in imitation of the Brunelleschi hospital across the square, to accommodate the Servite priests who worked there. The plainness of some rooms reflects something of the building's history, but all are decorated with fine fabrics and antiques, and look out either onto the piazza or peaceful gardens to the rear: top-floor rooms have glimpses of the Duomo. The five rooms in the nearby annexe, at Via dei Servi 49, are similarly styled, but the building doesn't have the same charisma. **€200**

MERLINI MAP p.72, POCKET MAP D3. Via Faenza 56 ☎ 055 212 848, Ⓦ hotelmerlini.it. Several budget hotels are crammed into this address, and the family-run *Merlini*, on the third floor (no lift), is one of the best. Its ten rooms have marble bathrooms – an unexpected bonus in this price bracket – and six give views of the Duomo. **€110**

MORANDI ALLA CROCETTA MAP p.72, POCKET MAP G3. Via Laura 50 ☎ 055 234 4747, Ⓦ hotelmorandi.it. An intimate three-star gem, whose small size and friendly welcome ensure a home-from-home atmosphere. Rooms are tastefully decorated with antiques and old prints, and vivid carpets laid on parquet floors. Two rooms have balconies opening onto a modest garden; another – with fresco fragments and medieval nooks and crannies – was converted from the site's former convent chapel. **€170**

MR. MY RESORT MAP p.72, POCKET MAP E2. Via delle Ruote 14a ☎ 055 283 955, Ⓦ mrflorence.it. Run by the same friendly family as *Relais Grand Tour* (see below), this luxury B&B has five bright, quirkily furnished rooms arranged around a tranquil garden, but the real draw is the private, stone-walled spa in the basement, complete with Turkish bath and jacuzzi. **€120**

Rooms for rent

To be classified as a hotel in Florence, a building has to have at least seven bedrooms. Places with fewer rooms operate as *affitacamere* ("rooms for rent") or *residenze d'epoca* (if occupying a historic building) – though, confusingly, a *residenza d'epoca* might have as many as a dozen rooms. Some *affitacamere* are just a couple of rooms in a private house, but several – and most *residenze d'epoca* – are small hotels in all but name, offering some of the most atmospheric accommodation in Florence. Many *affitacamere* are on the upper floors of large buildings, and can be reached only by stairs.

ORTO DE' MEDICI MAP p.72, POCKET MAP E3. Via San Gallo 30 ☎ 055 483 427, Ⓦ ortodeimedici.it. A 31-room frescoed and antique-furnished three-star, occupying a quiet palazzo in the university area. Via San Gallo is not the most attractive street in Florence, but the hotel has a nice formal garden and has been very impressively refurbished; its off-season rates are terrific too. €170

RELAIS GRAND TOUR MAP p.72, POCKET MAP E3. Via Santa Reparata 21 ☎ 055 283 955, Ⓦ florencegrandtour.com. The very hospitable owners have done a great job in turning two floors of this old palazzo, adjoining an eighteenth-century private theatre, into a superb guesthouse, with three large bedrooms upstairs and three suites on the ground floor. Each room is unique – one suite has Neapolitan majolica tiles in the bathroom, while another (formerly a dressing-room) is loaded with antique mirrors ("suitable for a couple", as the website has it). €150

RESIDENZA CASTIGLIONI MAP p.72, POCKET MAP D4. Via del Giglio 8 ☎ 055 239 6013, Ⓦ residenzacastiglioni.com. This discreet and hugely stylish hideaway has just half a dozen spacious en-suite double rooms (three of them frescoed), on the second floor of a palazzo very close to San Lorenzo church. Room 22 is the one to go for, with wall-to-wall frescoes. €170

RESIDENZA JOHANNA I MAP p.72, POCKET MAP E2. Via Bonifacio Lupi 14 ☎ 055 481 896, Ⓦ johanna.it. The longest-established of the *Johanna/Johlea* family of *residenze*, this genteel place is hidden away in an unmarked apartment building in a quiet, leafy corner of the city, a 5min walk north of San Marco. Rooms are cosy and well kept, and the management are as friendly and helpful as you could hope for. €130

East of the centre

DALÌ MAP p.90, POCKET MAP F5. Via dell'Oriuolo 17 ☎ 055 234 0706, Ⓦ hoteldali .com. One of the least expensive one-star options close to the centre, with just nine rooms, five with bath. The rooms are plain and rather basic, but the location – on the top floor of a palazzo built in 1492 – helps, as does the view from the back rooms of

the giant magnolia in the garden below. The friendly owners speak good English. €90

J & J MAP p.90, POCKET MAP G5. Via di Mezzo 20 ☎ 055 263 12, Ⓦ jandjhotel .net. The bland exterior of this former fifteenth-century convent conceals a romantic nineteen-room four-star hotel. Some rooms are vast split-level affairs, but all have charm and are furnished with modern fittings and a few antiques. Common areas are decked with flowers, and retain frescoes and vaulted ceilings from the original building. In summer, breakfast is served in the convent's lovely old cloister. €200

RELAIS SANTA CROCE MAP p.90, POCKET MAP F6. Via Ghibellina 87 ☎ 055 234 2230, Ⓦ relaissantacroce.com. This magnificent five-star shares a lobby with the mind-blowingly expensive *Pinchiorri* restaurant, and is a similarly top-flight establishment. The grandiose public rooms are a very slick amalgam of the historic and the contemporary, with modern sofas set on acres of gleaming parquet, surrounded by eighteenth-century stucco panels. Contemporary and understated luxury prevails in the bedrooms, which are graded "superior", "deluxe" and "exclusive" (these have their own saunas). Then there are suites, which are in the "if you have to ask the price you can't afford it" category. €420

Oltrarno

AD ASTRA MAP p.102. POCKET MAP B7. Via del Campuccio 53 ☎ 055 075 0602, Ⓦ adastraflorence.it. The spectacular Ad Astra is more a super-deluxe B&B than a hotel (it's unstaffed between 8pm and 8am), consisting of just nine luxurious rooms, seven of which are on the ground floor of the ancestral home of the Torrigiani family (the Marchese is still in residence), with two more in an annexe in the garden, which is said to be the largest private garden in Europe. Some of the rooms open onto the huge terrace that wraps around the building, and each has been individually designed. There are plenty of antiques around the place, as you'd expect, but many of the bedroom furnishings are the work of post-war Italian designers. €300

ANNALENA MAP p.102, POCKET MAP B8. Via Romana 34 ☎ 055 222 402, Ⓦ annalenahotel.com. A short way beyond Palazzo Pitti (and right by an entrance to the Bóboli gardens), this bargain twenty-room three-star occupies part of a building once owned by the Medici. The best rooms open onto a gallery with garden views, and a sprinkling of antiques lends a hint of old-world charm. **€100**

LA SCALETTA MAP p.102, POCKET MAP D7. Via Guicciardini 13 ☎ 055 283 028, Ⓦ lascaletta.com. Some of the rooms in this tidy and recently refurbished sixteen-room three-star give views across to the Bóboli gardens; those on the Via Guiccardini side are double-glazed against the traffic. Drinks are served on the rooftop terraces, where you look across the Bóboli in one direction and the city in the other. All rooms are en suite and nicely decorated in creamy tones. **€130**

PALAZZO GUADAGNI MAP p.102, POCKET MAP C7. Piazza Santo Spirito 9 ☎ 055 265 8376, Ⓦ palazzoguadagni.com. This very attractive three-star hotel has 15 rooms on three floors, furnished with family antiques. The middle floor is nicest, particularly room 10, with its frescoed ceiling. The lovely loggia gets the evening sun – the perfect place to wind down with an *aperitivo*. **€150**

TORRE DI BELLOSGUARDO MAP p.102. POCKET MAP A8. Via Roti Michelozzi 2 ☎ 055.229.8145, Ⓦ torrebellosguardo .com. It's not central – it's perched on a hill about 2km from the heart of Oltrarno – but the four-star Bellosguardo is one of the most beautiful hotels in the city. Dating back to the thirteenth century, and once home to Galileo, it's girdled by magnificent gardens (with a pool). Each of its 16 rooms (all uniquely and exquisitely furnished) is palatial. **From €300**

Hostels

ACADEMY HOSTEL MAP p.28, POCKET MAP E4. Via Ricasoli 9 ☎ 055 239 8665, Ⓦ academyhostel.eu. Since opening in 2008, this modern hostel has won awards for its service and excellent facilities: set in a seventeenth-century palazzo, it offers airy, high-ceilinged rooms (from singles to six beds) and a common area with huge flat-screen TV, book and DVD library and lots of computer terminals, plus a sunny terrace. All this, and an unbeatable location – just steps from the Duomo. Breakfast included. **Price per person per night from €34**

ARCHI ROSSI MAP p.72, POCKET MAP D3. Via Faenza 94r ☎ 055 290 804, Ⓦ hostelarchirossi.com. A 5min walk from the train station, this privately owned hostel is spotlessly clean and decorated with guests' wall-paintings and graffiti. It's popular – the 140 beds fill up quickly – and has a pleasant garden and terrace. There are some basic en-suite doubles too (on the third floor; no lift), and a restaurant serving cheap meals. Breakfast included. **Dorm beds from €30, double rooms from €90**

SANTA MONICA MAP p.102, POCKET MAP B6. Via Santa Monaca 6 ☎ 055 268 338, Ⓦ ostello.it. This privately owned hostel in Oltrarno has 112 beds, arranged in a dozen dorms (female-only and mixed) with between two and twenty beds. Kitchen facilities, laundry and free internet; meals are available but are not included. Check-in 6am–2am; lock-out 10am–2pm. Curfew 2am. It's a 10min walk from the station, or take bus #11, #36 or #37 to the second stop after the bridge. **Dorm beds from €22**

VILLA CAMERATA MAP p.121, POCKET MAP H2. Viale Augusto Righi 2–4 ☎ 055 601 451, Ⓦ ostellofirenze.it. Buses #11 from the station. This HI hostel in a beautiful park 5km northeast of the city is one of Europe's most attractive hostels, a sixteenth-century house with frescoed ceilings. There are 322 beds, and a few private rooms. Films in English are shown every night. Breakfast is included, but there are no kitchen facilities; dinner costs around €12. Check-in from 2pm. **Dorm beds from €20**

WOW FLORENCE HOSTEL MAP p.72, POCKET MAP F2. Via Venezia 18b ☏ 055 579 603, Ⓦ wowflorence.com. The WOW occupies part of an unlovely 1960s block, and the decor is a bit on the garish side, but it's well located (just a few minutes' walk north of San Marco), it's in good shape (having been fully refurbished a couple of years ago) and it's inexpensive. Wow has a good range of rooms, with singles, doubles and small dorms for groups of 4, 6 and 8, all furnished with IKEA-style kit. Every room has its own bathroom, and wifi is free, as is the buffet breakfast. There's a laundry on site, and no curfew. Not surprisingly, given Florence's dearth of budget accommodation, the WOW is popular – if you're coming in summer, you'll need to book months ahead. **Dorm beds from €35 (summer), double rooms from €100.**

Camping

CAMPING PANORAMICO MAP p.124, POCKET MAP H1. Via Peramondo 1, Fiesole ☏ 055 559 069, Ⓦ florencecamping.com. Located in Fiesole, this 120-pitch three-star site has a bar, restaurant, pool and small supermarket. There's a campsite nearer to the city centre, by Piazzale Michelangelo, but the Fiesole one is much preferable. Mid-March to Dec. **From €7 per person, plus €6 per tent.**

ESSENTIALS

Arrival

Your point of arrival is most likely to be Santa Maria Novella train station, which is located within a few minutes' walk of the heart of the historic centre: rail and bus connections from the three airports that serve the city all terminate at the station, as do international trains and buses from all over Italy.

Pisa airport

Most flights to Tuscany use Pisa's **Galileo Galilei** airport (☎ 050 849 300, ⓦ pisa-airport.com), 95km west of Florence and 3km from the centre of Pisa. The automated Pisa Mover rail shuttle, connecting the airport to Pisa Centrale station, runs every 5–8min, from 6am to midnight every day (€2.70); the journey takes little more than 5min. Alternatively, you can take the cheaper but rather less frequent and somewhat slower LAM Rossa city bus (€1.20) to Pisa Centrale; it leaves from in front of the Arrivals hall. The last train from Pisa Centrale to Florence is at 10.30pm, with services resuming at around 4.15am; the fare is €8.50. The Terravision direct bus service to Florence was suspended when we went to press; the rival Airport Bus Express runs regularly (€10 single), and takes an hour, if traffic is light; at busy times it can take 90min. The ticket office and bus stand is to the right as you come out of Arrivals.

Perètola airport

A few airlines use Florence's small Perètola (Amerigo Vespucci) airport (☎ 055 306 1300, ⓦ aeroporto.firenze .it), 5km northwest of the city centre. The Busitalia and ATAF bus companies operate a joint service from Perètola called Volainbus (ⓦ ataf.net), which provides half-hourly shuttles into the city from immediately outside the arrivals area. Tickets can be bought on board or from machines at the airport, and the journey takes about thirty minutes.

Bologna airport

A few airlines use Bologna (ⓦ bologna -airport.it) as a *gateway* airport for Florence. Aerobus shuttles depart every twenty minutes (5.30am–midnight) from outside the airport's Terminal A to Bologna's main train station (about 25min), from where regular trains run to Florence's Santa Maria Novella station in about an hour. Note, however, that Ryanair services to Bologna in fact fly to Forlì airport, which is more than 60km southeast of Bologna, and very inconvenient for Florence.

The train station

Florence's central station, Santa Maria Novella ("Firenze SMN" on timetables), is located just north of the church and square of Santa Maria Novella, a few blocks west of the Duomo. In the station are an accommodation service, left-luggage facilities and a 24-hour pharmacy. While in and around the station, you should keep a close eye on your bags at all times: it's a prime hunting-ground for thieves and pickpockets. Also avoid the concourse's various taxi and hotel touts, however friendly they may appear.

Getting around

Within the historic centre, walking is generally the most efficient way of getting around, and nowadays walking is a lot more pleasant than it used to be, with the extension of the **zona a traffico limitato** (ZTL) – which limits traffic in the centre to residents' cars, delivery vehicles and public transport – to cover most of the city centre from the river to a few blocks north of the Duomo.

Buses

If you want to cross town in a hurry, or visit some of the peripheral sights, your best option is to use one of the frequent and speedy **ATAF** buses (w ataf.net). Tickets are valid for unlimited journeys within a period of 90min (€1.20; €2 if bought on board), 24hr (€5) or 72hr (€12). You can save money with the ATAF electronic card called the **Carnet Agile**, which comes in three versions: the €10 card gives the equivalent of ten 90min tickets; the €20 card is equivalent to 21; and the €30 card is equivalent to 35. You can buy tickets from the main ATAF office inside Santa Maria Novella station (Mon–Sat 7am–8pm), from any shops and stalls displaying the ATAF sign, and from automatic machines all over Florence. Once you're on board, you must validate your ticket or card at the start of every journey. There's a hefty on-the-spot fine for any passenger without a validated ticket.

Taxis

You can't flag down a taxi in the street – you have to phone for one (t 055 4242, t 055 4798, t 055 4499 or t 055 4390) or go to a taxi rank; key locations include the train station, Piazza della Repubblica, Piazza del Duomo, Piazza Santa Maria Novella, Piazza San Marco, Piazza Santa Croce and Piazza Santa Trìnita. If you order a cab by phone, you'll be given the car's code name – usually a town, city or country – and its number, both of which are emblazoned on the vehicle. All rides are metered; at the start of the journey the meter should be set at €3.30, €5.30 if it's a Sunday or public holiday, or €6.60 between 10pm and 6am. Supplements are payable for journeys outside the city limits (to Fiesole, for example), and for each piece of luggage placed in the boot (€1).

Directory A–Z

Banks

Florence's main bank branches are around Piazza della Repubblica, but exchange booths (*cambio*) and ATM cash-card machines (*bancomat*) for Visa and MasterCard advances can be found across the city. Banks generally open Mon–Fri 8.20am–3.35pm.

Consulates

The UK consulate for northern Italy is at Via San Paolo 7, Milan t 02 723 001; the US has a consulate in Florence, at Lungarno Amerigo Vespucci 38 t 055 266 951.

Electricity

The supply in Italy is 220V, but anything requiring 240V will work. Most plugs have two round pins, so UK equipment will need an adapter. US equipment requires a transformer as well.

The Tramvia

The first line of the city's beleaguered Tramvia tram system was completed in 2010, but it's a commuter line that's of no use to tourists. In May 2014 it was announced that money had been found to resume work on lines T2 (from Piazza della Libertà to Perètola airport, via San Marco, the Duomo and Santa Maria Novella) and T3 (from Viale Strozzi to Careggi hospital). There is very strong resistance in the city to the idea of running a tramline past the Duomo, so revisions to the T2 route are likely.

Emergencies

Police ☎ 113, or ☎ 112 for the Carabinieri (military police); fire ☎ 115; ambulance ☎ 118. If your passport is lost or stolen, go to the police (see opposite) and report it to your consulate.

Health

The Medical Service is a private service used to dealing with foreigners; they have doctors on call 24hr a day on ☎ 055 475 411 (ⓦ medicalservice.firenze.it), or you can visit their clinic at Via Roma 4 (Mon–Fri 11am–noon & 5–6pm, Sat 11am–noon). Note that you'll need insurance cover to recoup the cost of a consultation, which will be at least €60. Florence's central hospital is on Piazza Santa Maria Nuova.

Internet access

Internet Train has branches at Borgo San Jacopo 30r, Via Guelfa 54–56r and Via Porta Rossa 38r (all Mon–Sat 10am–midnight, Sun 3–11pm; ⓦ internettrain.it). The tourist office has a full list of current internet points. Many hotels (and all of the pricier ones) offer free internet access.

Left luggage

The left luggage office is at Santa Maria Novella station, by platform 16 (daily 6am–midnight).

Lost property

Lost property handed in at the city or railway police ends up at Via Veracini 5 (Mon, Wed & Fri 9am–12.30pm, Tues & Thurs 9am–12.30pm & 2.30–4.30pm; ☎ 055 334 802; bus #17, #29, #30 or #35).

Museum admission

All of Florence's state-run museums belong to an association called Firenze Musei (ⓦ firenzemusei.it), which sets aside a daily quota of tickets that can be reserved in advance. The Uffizi, the Accademia and the Bargello belong to this group, as do the Palazzo Pitti museums, the Bóboli gardens, the Medici chapels in San Lorenzo, the archeological museum and the San Marco museum. The best source of online info for all of these museums is ⓦ uffizi.firenze.it.

You can **reserve tickets** (booking fee of €4 for Uffizi and Accademia, €3 for the rest) by phoning ☎ 055 294 883 (Mon–Fri 8.30am–6.30pm, Sat 8.30am–12.30pm), online at ⓦ firenzemusei.it and ⓦ uffizi.firenze.it, at the Firenze Musei booth at Orsanmichele (Mon–Sat 10am–4.15pm), at the My Accademia bookshop at Via Ricasoli 105r (Tues–Sun 8.15am–5pm) and at the museums themselves, in the case of the Uffizi and Pitti. If you book by phone, an English-speaking operator will allocate you a ticket for a specific hour, to be collected at the museum at a specific time, shortly before entry. That's the

Florentine addresses

Note that there is a **double address system** in Florence, one for businesses and one for all other properties – that, at least, is the theory, though in fact the distinction is far from rigorous. Business addresses are followed by the letter r (for *rosso*) and are marked on the building with a red number on a white plate, sometimes with an r after the numeral, but not always. The two series are independent of each other, which means that no. 20, for example, may be a long way from no. 20r.

Firenze Card

The Firenze Card, costing €72, is valid for 72 hours from the first time you use it, and gives access to 72 museums and monuments in greater Florence (including all the big ones), plus unlimited use of public transport. It also enables you to bypass the queues at the major museums, which have separate gates for card holders. You do, though, have to pack a hell of a lot into each day to make it worthwhile – for most people the 72 hours would be better spent getting the most out of a few sights, rather than racing around the city trying to justify the investment. What's more, some of the museums, such as Medici villa at Cerreto Guidi, are some distance out of the city, and are highly unlikely to feature on anyone's three-day blitz. The card can be bought at the Via Cavour and Piazza Stazione tourist offices, and at the Uffizi (door 2), Palazzo Vecchio, Bargello, Palazzo Pitti, Palazzo Strozzi, Museo Bardini and Cappella Brancacci; if bought online, at Ⓦ firenzecard.it, it can be collected at any of the tourist offices, or at the Museo Bardini, Cappella Brancacci, Palazzo Vecchio or Palazzo Strozzi.

theory, but in reality the line tends to be engaged for long periods at a stretch. Generally, the Orsanmichele booth – which is set into the wall of the church on the Via Calzaiuoli side – is the easiest option. Pre-booking is strongly recommended in summer for the Uffizi and the Accademia, whose allocation of reservable tickets is often sold out many days ahead.

Note that on-the-door admission to all state-run museums is free on the first Sunday of the month and for EU citizens under 18, on presentation of a passport; 18–25s get a fifty percent discount, as do teachers, on proof of identity. Nearly all of Florence's major museums are routinely **closed on Monday**, though some are open for a couple of Mondays each month. In the majority of cases, museum ticket offices close thirty minutes before the museum itself. At the Palazzo Vecchio and Museo Stibbert, however, it's one hour before, while at the Uffizi, Bargello, Museo dell'Opera del Duomo, the dome of the Duomo, the Campanile and Pitti museums it's 45 minutes.

For Florence's civic museums – of which the main ones are the Museo Bardini, Museo Santa Maria Novella, Palazzo Vecchio and the Cappella Brancacci – the website is Ⓦ museicivicifiorentini.it.comune.fi.it.

Pharmacies

The Farmacia Comunale, at the train station, is open 24hr. All'Insegna del Moro, at Piazza San Giovanni 20r, on the north side of the Baptistery, and Farmacia Molteni, at Via dei Calzaiuoli 7r, alternate their 24hr service every two weeks. All pharmacies display a late-night roster in their window.

Police

Emergency ☏ 112 or 113. To report a theft or other crime, go to the Carabinieri at Borgo Ognissanti 48, to the Questura at Via Zara 2 (both 24hr), or to the tourist police at Via Pietrapiana 50r (Mon–Fri 8.30am–6.30pm, Sat closes 1.30pm) – you're more likely to find an English-speaker at the last of these. If you do report a theft or other crime, you will have to fill out a form (una denuncia); this may be time-consuming, but it's essential if you

Florence online

Agenzia per il Turismo di Firenze Ⓦ www.firenzeturismo.it. The official tourist office site, with an English-language option. Useful for information on forthcoming exhibitions and hotel listings.

Firenze Spettacolo Ⓦ firenzespettacolo.it. The online edition of Florence's listings magazine.

Musei Civici Ⓦ museicivicifiorentini.it. Information on Florence's civic museums.

want to make a claim on your travel insurance on returning home.

Post office

The main central post office is near Piazza della Repubblica at Via Pelliceria 3 (Mon–Fri 8.15am–7pm, Sat 8.15am–12.30pm). If all you want are stamps (*francobolli*), then it's easier to buy them at one of the city's innumerable tabacchi, which are marked by a sign outside with a white "T" on a blue background.

Telephones

Nearly all of Florence's public call-boxes accept coins, but you get more time for your euros if you use a phone card, which can be bought from any tabacchi and any shop displaying the Telecom Italia sticker. You're never far from a pay phone – every sizeable piazza has at least one.

Time

Italy is on Central European Time (CET), one hour ahead of the UK, six hours ahead of Eastern Standard Time and nine hours ahead of Pacific Standard Time.

Tourist information

The main tourist office is at Via Cavour 1r, a 5min walk north of the Duomo (Mon–Sat 9am–1pm; ☏ 055 290 832, Ⓦ firenzeturismo.it); this office provides information not just on the city but on the whole of Florence province. Local government spending cuts have led to a drastic curtailment of its opening hours; it's possible that more helpful hours will be restored in the future. Smaller offices are in the Loggia del Bigallo, by the Baptistery (Mon–Sat 9am–7pm, Sun 9am–2pm; ☏ 055 288 496), and opposite the train station, at Piazza della Stazione 4 (Mon–Sat 9am–7pm, Sun 9am–2pm; ☏ 055 212 245).

Another excellent source of information is *Firenze Spettacolo* (Ⓦ firenzespettacolo.it; €2), a monthly, mostly bilingual listings magazine available from bookshops and larger newsstands. Also useful is *The Florentine* (Ⓦ theflorentine.net), a free bi-weekly English-language paper, available at the tourist office, most bookshops and various other spots (the website lists all of the places it can be picked up).

Festivals and events

Scoppio del Carro

Easter Sunday

For Easter Sunday's Scoppio del Carro (Explosion of the Cart), a cartload of fireworks is hauled by six white oxen from the Porta a Prato to the Duomo; there, during the midday Mass, the whole lot is set off by a "dove" that whizzes down a wire from the high altar.

Festa del Grillo

First Sunday after Ascension

On the first Sunday after Ascension Day (forty days after Easter), the Festa del Grillo (Festival of the Cricket) is held in the Cascine park. In among the market stalls and the picnickers, people sell tiny mechanical crickets. Live crickets were sold until recently, a vestige of a ritual that may hark back to the days when farmers had to scour their land for locusts.

Maggio Musicale Fiorentino

May–June

Ⓦ **maggiofiorentino.com**

Confusingly, the Maggio Musicale isn't restricted to May (Maggio), but lasts for a couple of months from late April or early May. The festival has its own orchestra, chorus and ballet company, plus guest appearances from foreign ensembles. Events are staged at the Teatro Comunale (or its Teatro Piccolo), the Teatro della Pergola, the Palazzo dei Congressi, the Teatro Verdi, the Opera di Firenze and occasionally in the Bóboli gardens. Information and tickets can be obtained from the Teatro Comunale, Corso Italia 16.

Estate Fiesolana

July–August

Much smaller and less exclusive than the Maggio Musicale, concentrating more on chamber and symphonic music, the Estate Fiesolana is held in Fiesole every summer, usually from July to late August. Films and theatre are also featured, and most events are held in the Teatro Romano.

St John's Day and the Calcio Storico

June 24 and two later dates

The saint's day of John the Baptist, Florence's patron, is June 24 – the occasion for a massive fireworks display up on Piazzale Michelangelo, and for the Calcio Storico. Played in sixteenth-century costume, this uniquely Florentine mayhem is a three-match series culminating with the final on June 24, in Piazza Santa Croce. Each of the four historic quarters fields a team of 27 players, Santa Croce playing in blue, San Giovanni in green, Santa Maria Novella in red and Santo Spirito in impractical white. The prize for the winning side is a vast quantity of steak, equivalent to the white calf traditionally awarded to the victors. A sort of hybrid of rugby, boxing and wrestling, the game is characterized by incomprehensible rules and an extraordinary degree of violence.

Festa delle Rificolone

September 7

The Festa delle Rificolone (Festival of the Lanterns) takes place on the Virgin's birthday, September 7, with a procession of children from Santa Croce to Piazza Santissima Annunziata, where market stalls are set out for the evening. Each child carries a coloured paper lantern with a candle inside it – a throwback to the days when people from the surrounding countryside would troop by lantern light into the city for the Feast of the Virgin.

National holidays

Everything, except some bars and restaurants, closes on Italy's official **national holidays**, which are: January 1, January 6 (Epiphany), Easter Monday, April 25 (Liberation Day), May 1 (Labour Day), June 2 (Day of the Republic), August 15 (Ferragosto; Assumption), November 1 (Ognissanti; All Saints), December 8 (Immaculate Conception), December 25, December 26.

Chronology

Eighth century BC The Etruscans are settled throughout the area known as Tuscany, with their principal settlements in Roselle, Vetulonia, Populonia, Volterra, Chiusi, Cortona, Arezzo and – most northerly of all – Fiesole.

59 BC The Roman colony of Florentia is established by Julius Caesar as a settlement for army veterans. By now the Romans have either subsumed or exterminated most Etruscan towns.

Second and third centuries AD Rapid expansion of Florentia as a river port.

Fourth century AD Christianity is spreading throughout Italy. The church of San Lorenzo and the martyr's shrine at San Miniato are both established in Florentia.

552 Florence falls to the hordes of the Gothic king Totila. Less than twenty years later the Lombards storm in, subjugating the city to the duchy whose capital was in Pavia.

End of the eighth century Charlemagne's Franks have taken control of much of Italy, with the administration overseen by imperial margraves, based in Lucca. These proxy rulers develop into some of the most powerful figures in the Holy Roman Empire and are instrumental in spreading Christianity even further.

978 Willa, widow of the margrave Uberto, establishes the Badìa in Florence, the first monastic foundation in the centre of the city.

1027 The position of margrave passes to the Canossa family, who take the title of the Counts of Tuscia (as Tuscany was then called). The most influential figure produced by this dynasty is Matilda, daughter of the first Canossa margrave.

1115 In the year of Matilda's death she grants Florence the status of an independent city. The new commune of Florence is essentially governed by a council of one hundred men, the great majority drawn from the rising merchant class. In 1125 the city's increasing dominance of the region is confirmed when it crushes the rival city of Fiesole. Fifty years later, as the population booms with the rise of the textile industry, new walls are built around what is now one of the largest cities in Europe.

Thirteenth century Throughout Tuscany, conflict develops between the Ghibelline faction and the Guelphs – the former, broadly speaking, are pro-empire, with the Guelphs defined chiefly by their loyalty to the papacy. When Charles of Anjou conquers Naples in 1266, association with the anti-imperial French becomes another component of Guelphism, and a loose Guelph alliance soon stretches from Paris to Naples, substantially funded by the bankers of Tuscany. Florence and Lucca are generally Guelph strongholds, while Pisa, Arezzo, Prato, Pistoia and Siena tend to side with the empire.

1207 Florence's governing council is replaced by the *podestà*, an executive official who is traditionally a non-Florentine. Around this time the first *arti* (guilds) are formed to promote the interests of the traders and bankers.

1248 Florence's Ghibellines enlist the help of Emperor Frederick II to oust the Guelphs, but within two years they have been displaced by the Guelph-backed regime of the Primo Popolo, a quasi-democratic government drawn from the mercantile class.

1280 Power passes to the Secondo Popolo, a regime run by the Arti Maggiori (Great Guilds). The fulcrum of power in Florence shifts definitively towards its bankers, merchants and manufacturers.

1293 The Secondo Popolo excludes the nobility from government and invests power in the Signoria, a council drawn from the Arti Maggiori.

1348 The Black Death destroys as many as half the city's population. However, the plague is equally devastating throughout the region, and does nothing to reverse the economic and political supremacy of the city.

1406 Florence takes control of Pisa and thus gains a long-coveted seaport. Despite the survival of Sienese independence into the sixteenth century, the history of Tuscany increasingly becomes the history of Florence.

1431–1434 Cosimo de' Medici is imprisoned by the city authorities, having provoked the big families of the Signoria with his support for the members of the disenfranchised lesser guilds. In 1434, after a session of the Parlamento – a general council called in times of emergency – he is invited to return. Having secured the military support of the Sforza family of Milan, Cosimo (Cosimo il Vecchio) becomes the pre-eminent figure in the city's political life for more than three decades. Florence's reputation as the most innovative cultural centre in Europe is strengthened by his patronage of Donatello, Michelozzo and a host of other artists.

1439 Council of Florence is convened, to try to reconcile the Catholic and Eastern churches. The consequent influx of Greek scholars adds momentum to the study of classical philosophy and literature.

1478 The Pazzi family conspire with Pope Sixtus IV to murder Lorenzo il Magnifico (Cosimo's grandson, and the de facto ruler of Florence) and his brother Giuliano; the plot fails, and only increases the esteem in which Lorenzo is held.

1494 Lorenzo's son Piero is obliged to flee Florence following his surrender to the invading French army of Charles VIII. This invasion is the commencement of a bloody half-century dominated by the so-called Wars of Italy.

1498 Having in effect ruled the city in the absence of the Medici, the Dominican friar Girolamo Savonarola is executed as a heretic.

1512 Following Florence's defeat by the Spanish and papal armies, the Medici return, in the person of the vicious Giuliano, Duke of Nemours.

1527 Holy Roman Emperor Charles V's army pillages Rome. The humiliation of Pope Clement VII (a Medici) spurs the people of Florence to eject his deeply unpopular relatives.

1530 After a siege by the combined papal and imperial forces, Florence is obliged to receive Alessandro, who was proclaimed Duke of Florence, the first Medici to bear the title of ruler.

1537 Alessandro is assassinated and power passes to another Cosimo (not a direct heir but rather a descendant of Cosimo il Vecchio's brother), thanks to support from the emperor Charles V, whose daughter was married to Alessandro.

1557 Cosimo buys the territory of Siena from the Habsburgs, giving Florence control of all of Tuscany with the solitary exception of Lucca. Two years later Florentine hegemony in Tuscany is confirmed in the Treaty of Cateau-Cambrésis, the final act in the Wars of Italy.

1570 Cosimo takes the title Cosimo I, Grand Duke of Tuscany. In European terms Tuscany is a second-rank power, but it's one of the strongest states in Italy. Cosimo builds the Uffizi, extends and overhauls the Palazzo Vecchio, installs the Medici in the Palazzo Pitti, has the Ponte Santa Trìnita constructed across the Arno and commissions much of the public sculpture around the Piazza della Signoria. His descendants remain in power until 1737.

1630s The market for Florence's woollen goods collapses, and the city's banks go into a terminal slump.

1737 Under the terms of a treaty signed by Anna Maria de' Medici (the sister of Gian Gastone de' Medici, the last male Medici), Florence passes to the House of Lorraine, cousins of the Austrian Habsburgs.

1799 Napoleon dislodges the Austrians from Italy, but after his fall from power the Lorraine dynasty is brought back, remaining in residence until the last of the line, Leopold II, consents to his own deposition in 1859.

1865 Florence becomes the capital of the new Kingdom of Italy, a position it holds until 1870, when Rome takes over. The city's subsequent decline is accelerated by the economic disruption that follows World War I.

1943 After the Allied landing at Monte Cassino, Tuscany is a battlefield between the Nazis and the partisans. Substantial parts of Florence are wrecked by the retreating German army, who bomb all the bridges except the Ponte Vecchio and blow up much of the medieval city near the banks of the Arno.

Since World War II After World War II the province of Florence establishes itself as the third largest industrial centre in Italy. Textiles, metalwork, glass, ceramics, pharmaceuticals and chemical production remain major industries in the province, while in Florence itself many long-established crafts continue to thrive, notably jewellery and gold-working, the manufacture of handmade paper, perfumery and leatherwork. But tourism is the mainstay of Florence's economy, with around ten million overnight stays per year, a number that rises annually.

Italian

What follows is a brief pronunciation guide and a run down of essential words and phrases. For more detail, get Italian: Rough Guide Phrasebook.

Pronunciation

Italian **pronunciation** is easy, since every word is spoken exactly as it is written. The only difficulties you are likely to encounter are the few consonants that are different from English:

c before e or i is pronounced as in **ch**urch, while **ch** before the same vowels is hard, as in **c**at.

sci or **sce** are pronounced as in **sh**eet and **sh**elter respectively.

g is soft before **e** and **i**, as in **g**eranium; hard when followed by **h**, as in **g**arlic.

gn has the ni sound of our "o**ni**on".

gl in Italian is softened to something like li in English, as in sta**lli**on.

h is not aspirated, as in **h**onour.

Nearly all Italian words are stressed on the penultimate syllable unless an accent (´ or `) denotes otherwise, although written accents are often left out in practice. Note that the ending -ia or -ie counts as two syllables, hence *trattoria* is stressed on the i.

Words and phrases

Basic words and phrases

Good morning	Buongiorno
Good afternoon/ evening	Buonasera
Good night	Buonanotte
Goodbye	Arrivederci
Yes	Sì
No	No
Please	Per favore
Thank you (very much)	Grazie (molte/ mille grazie)
You're welcome	Prego
Alright/that's OK	Va bene

How are you?	Come stai/sta? (informal/formal)
I'm fine	Bene
Do you speak English?	Parla inglese?
I don't understand	Non ho capito
I don't know	Non lo so
Excuse me	Mi scusi/Prego
Excuse me (in a crowd)	Permesso
I'm sorry	Mi dispiace
I'm English	Sono inglese
Scottish	scozzese
American	americano
Irish	irlandese
Welsh	gallese
Today	Oggi
Tomorrow	Domani
Day after tomorrow	Dopodomani
Yesterday	Ieri
Now	Adesso
Later	Più tardi
Wait a minute!	Aspetta!
In the morning	Di mattina
In the afternoon	Nel pomeriggio
In the evening	Di sera
Here/there	Qui/Là
Good/bad	Buono/Cattivo
Big/small	Grande/Piccolo
Cheap/expensive	Economico/Caro
Hot/cold	Caldo/Freddo
Near/far	Vicino/Lontano
Vacant/occupied	Libero/Occupato
With/without	Con/Senza
More/less	Più/Meno
Enough, no more	Basta
Mr...	Signor...
Mrs...	Signora...
Miss...	Signorina... (il Signor, la Signora, la Signorina when speaking about someone else)

Numbers

1	uno
2	due
3	tre
4	quattro
5	cinque
6	sei
7	sette

8	otto
9	nove
10	dieci
11	undici
12	dodici
13	tredici
14	quattordici
15	quindici
16	sedici
17	diciassette
18	diciotto
19	diciannove
20	venti
21	ventuno
22	ventidue
30	trenta
40	quaranta
50	cinquanta
60	sessanta
70	settanta
80	ottanta
90	novanta
100	cento
101	centuno
110	centodieci
200	duecento
500	cinquecento
1000	mille
5000	cinquemila
10,000	diecimila
50,000	cinquantamila

Some signs

Entrata/Uscita	Entrance/exit
Aperto/Chiuso	Open/closed
Arrivi/Partenze	Arrivals/departures
Chiuso per restauro	Closed for restoration
Chiuso per ferie	Closed for holidays
Tirare/Spingere	Pull/push
Non toccare	Do not touch
Pericolo	Danger
Attenzione	Beware
Pronto soccorso	First aid
Vietato fumare	No smoking

Transport

Traghetto	Ferry
Autostazione	Bus station
Stazione ferroviaria	Train station
Un biglietto a ...	A ticket to ...
Solo andata/ andata e ritorno	One-way/return
A che ora parte?	What time does it leave?
Da dove parte?	Where does it leave from?

Accommodation

Albergo	Hotel
Ha una camera...	Do you have a room...
per una/due/ tre person(a/e)	for one/two/ three people
per una/due/ tre nott(e/i) con un letto matrimoniale	for one/two/ three nights with a double bed
con una doccia/ un bagno	with a shower/bath
Quanto costa?	How much is it?
È compresa la prima colazione?	Is breakfast included?
Ha niente che costa di meno?	Do you have any-thing cheaper?
La prendo	I'll take it
Vorrei prenotare una camera	I'd like to book a room
Ho una prenotazione	I have a booking
Ostello per la gioventù	Youth hostel

In the restaurant

Una tavola	A table
Vorrei prenotare una tavola per due alle otto	I'd like to book a table for two people at eight o'clock
Abbiamo bisogno di un coltello	We need a knife
una forchetta	a fork
un cucchiaio	a spoon
un bicchiere	a glass
Che cosa mi consiglia lei?	What do you recommend?
Cameriere/a!	Waiter/waitress!
Il conto	Bill/check
È incluso il servizio?	Is service included?
Sono vegetariano/a	I'm a vegetarian

Questions and directions

Dove?	Where?
(Dov'è/Dove sono)?	(where is/are ...?)
Quando?	When?

Cosa? (Cos'è?)	What? (what is it?)
Quanto/Quanti?	How much/many?
Perché?	Why?
È/C'è È/C'è ...?)	It is/there is (is it/is there...?)
Che ora è/ Che ore sono?	What time is it?
Come arrivo a...?	How do I get to...?
A che ora apre?	What time does it open?
A che ora chiude?	What time does it close?
Quanto costa? (Quanto costano?)	How much does it cost ? (...do they cost?)
Come si chiama in italiano?	What's it called in Italian?

Menu reader

Basics and snacks

Aceto	Vinegar
Aglio	Garlic
Biscotti	Biscuits
Burro	Butter
Caramelle	Sweets
Cioccolato	Chocolate
Focaccia	Oven-baked bread-based snack
Formaggio	Cheese
Frittata	Omelette
Gelato	Ice cream
Grissini	Bread sticks
Marmellata	Jam
Olio	Oil
Olive	Olives
Pane	Bread
Pane integrale	Wholemeal bread
Panino	Bread roll
Patatine	Crisps
Patatine fritte	Chips
Pepe	Pepper
Pizzetta	Small cheese and tomato pizza
Riso	Rice
Sale	Salt
Tramezzini	Sandwich
Uova	Eggs
Yogurt	Yoghurt
Zucchero	Sugar
Zuppa	Soup

Starters (Antipasti)

Antipasto misto	Mixed cold meats and cheese (and a selection of other things in this list)
Caponata	Mixed aubergine, olives, tomatoes and celery
Caprese	Tomato and mozzarella salad
Crostini di milza	Minced spleen on pieces of toast
Donzele/donzelline	Fried dough balls
Fettuna/bruschetta	Garlic toast with olive oil
Finocchiona	Pork sausage flavoured with fennel
Insalata di mare	Seafood salad
Insalata di riso	Rice salad
Melanzane in parmigiana	Fried aubergine in tomato and parmesan cheese sauce
Mortadella	Salami-type cured meat
Pancetta	Bacon
Peperonata	Grilled green, red or yellow peppers stewed in olive oil
Pinzimonio	Raw seasonal vegetables in olive oil, with salt and pepper
Pomodori ripieni	Stuffed tomatoes
Prosciutto	Ham
Prosciutto di cinghiale	Cured wild boar ham
Salame	Salami
Salame toscano	Pork sausage with pepper and cubes of fat
Salsicce	Pork or wild boar sausage

The first course (Il primo)

Soups

Acquacotta	Onion soup served with toast and poached egg
Brodo	Clear broth

Cacciucco	Fish stew with tomatoes, bread and red wine
Carabaccia	Onion soup
Garmugia	Soup made with fava beans, peas, artichokes, asparagus and bacon
Minestra di farro	Wheat and bean soup
Minestrina	Any light soup
Minestrone	Thick vegetable soup
Minestrone alla fiorentina	Haricot bean soup with red cabbage, tomatoes, onions and herbs
Panzanella	Summer salad of tomatoes, basil, cucumber, onion and bread
Pappa al pomodoro	Tomato soup thickened with bread
Pasta e fagioli	Pasta soup with beans
Pastina in brodo	Pasta pieces in clear broth
Ribollita	Winter vegetable soup, based on beans and thickened with bread
Stracciatella	Broth with egg
Zuppa di fagioli	Bean soup

Pasta and gnocchi

Cannelloni	Large tubes of pasta, stuffed
Farfalle	Literally "bow"-shaped pasta; the word also means "butterflies"
Fettuccine	Narrow pasta ribbons
Gnocchi	Small potato and dough dumplings
Gnocchi di ricotta	Dumplings filled with ricotta and spinach
Lasagne	Lasagne
Maccheroni	Tubular spaghetti
Pappardelle (con lepre)	Wide, short noodles, often served with hare sauce
Pasta al forno	Pasta baked with minced meat, eggs, tomato and cheese
Pasta alla carrettiera	Pasta with tomato, garlic, pepper, parsley and chilli
Penne	Smaller version of rigatoni
Penne strasciate	Quill-shaped pasta in meat sauce
Ravioli	Small packets of stuffed pasta
Rigatoni	Large, grooved, tubular pasta
Risotto	Cooked rice dish, with sauce
Spaghetti	Spaghetti
Spaghettini	Thin spaghetti
Tagliatelle	Pasta ribbons; another word for fettucine
Tortellini	Small rings of pasta, stuffed with meat or cheese
Vermicelli	Very thin spaghetti (literally "little worms")

Pasta sauces

Aglio e olio (e peperoncino)	Tossed in garlic and olive oil (and hot chillies)
Arrabiata	Spicy tomato sauce
Bolognese	Meat sauce
Burro e salvia	Butter and sage
Carbonara	Cream, ham and beaten egg
Frutta di mare	Seafood
Funghi	Mushroom
Matriciana	Cubed pork and tomato sauce
Panna	Cream
Parmigiano	Parmesan cheese
Pesto	Ground basil, pine nut, garlic and pecorino sauce
Pomodoro	Tomato sauce
Ragù	Meat sauce
Vongole	Clam and tomato sauce

ITALIAN

The second course (Il secondo)

Meat (carne)

Agnello	Lamb
Arista	Roast pork loin with garlic and rosemary
Bistecca	Steak
Bistecca alla fiorentina	Thick grilled T-bone steak
Cibreo	Chicken liver and egg stew
Coniglio	Rabbit
Costolette	Chops
Cotolette	Cutlets
Fegatini	Chicken livers
Fegato	Liver
Involtini	Steak slices, rolled and stuffed
Lingua	Tongue
Lombatina	Veal chop
Maiale	Pork
Manzo	Beef
Ossobuco	Shin of veal
Peposo	Peppered beef stew
Pollo	Chicken
Pollo alla diavola/ al mattone	Chicken flattened with a brick, grilled with herbs
Polpette	Meatballs (or minced balls of anything)
Rognoni	Kidneys
Salsiccia	Sausage
Saltimbocca	Veal with ham
Scottiglia	Stew of veal, game and poultry, cooked with white wine and tomatoes
Spezzatino	Stew
Spiedini di maiale	Skewered spiced cubes of pork loin and liver, with bread and bay leaves
Tacchino	Turkey
Trippa	Tripe
Trippa alla fiorentina	Tripe in tomato sauce, served with parmesan
Vitello	Veal

Fish (pesce) and shellfish (crostacei)

Acciughe	Anchovies
Anguilla	Eel
Aragosta	Lobster
Baccalà alla livornese	Salt cod with garlic, tomatoes and parsley
Bronzino/Branzino	Sea bass
Calamari	Squid
Caparossoli	Shrimps
Cape sante	Scallops
Coda di rospo	Monkfish
Cozze	Mussels
Dentice	Dentex (like sea bass)
Gamberetti	Shrimps
Gamberi	Prawns
Granchio	Crab
Orata	Bream
Ostriche	Oysters
Pescespada	Swordfish
Polpo	Octopus
Rombo	Turbot
San Pietro	John Dory
Sarde	Sardines
Schie	Shrimps
Seppie	Cuttlefish
Sogliola	Sole
Tonno	Tuna
Tonno con fagioli	Tuna with white beans and raw onion
Triglie	Red mullet
Trota	Trout
Vongole	Clams

Vegetables (contorni) and salad (insalata)

Asparagi	Asparagus
Asparagi alla fiorentina	Asparagus with butter, fried egg and cheese
Basilico	Basil
Broccoli	Broccoli
Capperi	Capers
Carciofi	Artichokes
Carciofini	Artichoke hearts
Carotte	Carrots
Cavolfiori	Cauliflower
Cavolo	Cabbage
Ceci	Chickpeas
Cetriolo	Cucumber
Cipolla	Onion
Fagioli	Beans

Fagioli all'uccelletto	White beans cooked with tomatoes, garlic and sage
Fagiolini	Green beans
Finocchio	Fennel
Frittata di carciofi	Fried artichoke flan
Funghi	Mushrooms
Insalata verde/ insalata mista	Green salad/ mixed salad
Melanzana	Aubergine/eggplant
Patate	Potatoes
Peperoni	Peppers
Piselli	Peas
Pomodori	Tomatoes
Radicchio	Chicory
Spinaci	Spinach
Zucca	Pumpkin
Zucchini	Courgettes

Desserts (dolci)

Amaretti	Macaroons
Brigidini	Anise wafer biscuits
Buccellato	Anise raisin cake
Cantucci/cantuccini	Small almond biscuits, served with Vinsanto wine
Cassata	Ice cream cake with candied fruit
Castagnaccio	Unleavened chestnut-flour cake containing raisins, walnuts and rosemary
Cenci	Fried dough dusted with powdered sugar
Frittelle di riso	Rice fritters
Gelato	Ice cream
Macedonia	Fruit salad
Meringa	Frozen meringue with whipped cream and chocolate
Necci	Chestnut-flour crêpes
Panforte	Hard fruit, nut and spice cake
Ricciarelli	Marzipan almond biscuits
Schiacciata alla fiorentina	Orange-flavoured cake covered with powdered sugar, eaten at carnival time
Schiacciata con l'uva	Grape- and sugar-covered bread dessert
Torta	Cake, tart
Zabaglione	Dessert made with eggs, sugar and Marsala wine
Zuccotto	Sponge cake filled with chocolate and whipped cream
Zuppa Inglese	Trifle

Cheese (formaggi)

Caciocavallo	A type of dried, mature mozzarella cheese
Fontina	Northern Italian cheese used in cooking
Gorgonzola	Soft blue-veined cheese
Mozzarella	Bland, soft white cheese used on pizzas
Parmigiano	Parmesan
Pecorino	Strong-tasting hard sheep's cheese
Provolone	Hard strong cheese
Ricotta	Soft white cheese made from ewe's milk, used in sweet or savoury dishes

Fruit and nuts (frutta and noce)

Ananas	Pineapple
Arance	Oranges
Banane	Bananas
Ciliegie	Cherries
Fichi	Figs
Fragole	Strawberries
Limone	Lemon
Mandorle	Almonds
Mele	Apples
Melone	Melon
Pere	Pears
Pesche	Peaches
Pinoli	Pine nuts
Pistacchio	Pistachio nut
Uve	Grapes

Cooking terms

Affumicato	Smoked
Al dente	Firm, not overcooked
Al ferro	Grilled without oil
Al forno	Baked
Al Marsala	Cooked with Marsala wine
Al vapore	Steamed
Alla brace	Barbecued
Alla griglia	Grilled
Allo spiedo	On the spit
Arrosto	Roasted
Ben cotto	Well done
Bollito	Boiled
Brasato	Cooked in wine
Cotto	Cooked (not raw)
Crudo	Raw
Fritto	Fried
In umido	Stewed
Lesso	Boiled
Milanese	Fried in egg and breadcrumbs
Pizzaiola	Cooked with tomato sauce
Ripieno	Stuffed
Sangue	Rare
Surgelato	Frozen

Drinks

Acqua minerale	Mineral water
Alla spina	Draught (beer)
Aranciata	Orangeade
Bicchiere	Glass
Birra	Beer
Bottiglia	Bottle
Caffè	Coffee
Cioccolata calda	Hot chocolate
Ghiaccio	Ice
Granita	Iced coffee or fruit drink
Latte	Milk
Limonata	Lemonade
Selz	Soda water
Spremuta	Fresh fruit juice
Spumante	Sparkling wine
Succo	Concentrated fruit juice with sugar
Tè	Tea
Tonico	Tonic water
Vino	Wine
Rosso	Red
Bianco	White
Rosato	Rosé
Secco	Dry
Dolce	Sweet
Litro	Litre
Mezzo	Half
Quarto	Quarter
Salute!	Cheers!

SMALL PRINT

Publishing information

This 3rd edition published April 2018 by **Rough Guides Ltd**, Alpha House, 100 Borough High Street, London, SE1 1LB

Distribution

UK, Ireland and Europe
Apa Publications (UK) Ltd; sales@roughguides.com
United States and Canada
Ingram Publisher Services; ips@ingramcontent.com
Australia and New Zealand
Woodslane; info@woodslane.com.au
Southeast Asia
Apa Publications (SN) Pte; sales@roughguides.com
Worldwide
Apa Publications (UK) Ltd; sales@roughguides.com

Special sales, content licensing and co-publishing

Rough Guides can be purchased in bulk quantities at discounted prices. We can create special editions, personalized jackets and corporate imprints tailored to your needs. sales@roughguides.com

roughguides.com

Printed in China

164pp includes index
A catalogue record for this book is available from the British Library
ISBN 978-0-24130-648-2

The publishers and authors have done their best to ensure the accuracy and currency of all the information in **Pocket Rough Guide Florence**, however, they can accept no responsibility for any loss, injury, or inconvenience sustained by any traveller as a result of information or advice contained in the guide.
1 3 5 7 9 8 6 4 2

Rough Guides credits

Editor: Ros Walford
Layout: Nikhil Agarwal
Cartography: Edward Wright
Picture editor: Michelle Bhatia
Photographer: Diana Jarvis

Managing editor: Monica Woods
Cover photo research:
Sarah Stewart-Richardson
Original design: Richard Czapnik

Author: Jonathan Buckley (ⓦ jonathan-buckley.co.uk) has written and contributed to various Rough Guides. He has published ten novels, and in 2015 was the winner of the BBC National Short Story Award. He lives in Brighton.

Help us update

We've gone to a lot of effort to ensure that the third edition of the **Pocket Rough Guide to Florence** is accurate and up-to-date. However, things change – places get "discovered", opening hours are notoriously fickle, restaurants and rooms raise prices or lower standards. If you feel we've got it wrong or left something out, we'd like to know, and if you can remember the address, the price, the hours, the phone number, so much the better.

Please send your comments with the subject line "**Pocket Rough Guide Florence Update**" to mail@roughguides.com. We'll credit all contributions and send a copy of the next edition (or any other Rough Guide if you prefer) for the very best emails.

Photo credits

All photos © Rough Guides except the following:
(Key: t-top; c-centre; b-bottom; l-left; r-right)

Cover: Cathedral of Santa Maria del Fiore, Florence Old Town **Alamy:** Jan Wlodarczyk
Cover flap: Getty Images/Matej Divizna (t); Shutterstock/Agnieszka Mikosza (b)

p.1 Alamy Stock Photo/Alpineguide
p.2 Getty Images/Atlantide Phototravel/Corbis (cr); Getty Images/Julian Elliott Photography (bl); Dreamstime.com/Dani74 (br)
p.4 Getty Images/Corbis/Sylvain Sonnet
p.5 Alamy Stock Photo/Bailey-Cooper Photography
p.6 Alamy Stock Photo/Adam Eastland
p.10 SuperStock/Hemis.fr
p.11 Getty Images/Corbis/Sylvain Sonnet (tr)
p.12 SuperStock/Jose Antonio Moreno (t); p.12 SuperStock/DeAgostini (b)
p.14 Getty Images/Corbis/Sylvain Sonnet (t); Alamy Stock Photo/David South (b)
p.16 Alamy Stock Photo/robertharding (t)
p.17 Getty Images/Richard I'Anson (bl); Getty Images/Corbis/Sylvain Sonnet (br)
p.18 Getty Images/Gallo Images/Roger de la Harpe (cr)
p.19 Shutterstock.com/photogolfer (c)

p.21 Shutterstock/I Wei Huang (c)
p.22 Getty Images/Atlantide Phototravel (t); Alamy Stock Photo/Eddy Galeotti (c)
p.23 Museo Marino Marini/Dario Lasagni (t); Alamy Stock Photo/Adam Eastland (c)
p.32 Museo dell'Opera del Duomo Firenze/Claudio Giovannini
p.33 Museo Dell'Opera Del Duomo/Antonio Quattrone
p.34 Getty Images/Corbis Documentary/Sylvain Sonnet
p.39 Getty Images/De Agostini
p.40 Alamy Stock Photo/Sorin Colac
p.42 Getty Images/Sylvain Sonnet
p.43 Shutterstock.com/vvoe
p.54 Getty Images/Corbis/Ken Kaminesky
p.59 Alamy Stock Photo/MARKA
p.79 Alamy Stock Photo/Dennis MacDonald
p.82 Alamy Stock Photo/Alex Ramsay
p.88 Getty Images/Corbis Documentary / Sylvain Sonnet
p.97 Shutterstock/REX/imageBROKER / Otto Stadler
p.98 Caffe Italiano Osteria
p.110 Getty Images/Sergio Anelli
p.111 Alamy Stock Photo/Hemis

Index

Maps are marked in **bold**.

A

Accademia 16, 78
addresses, Florence 142
airports 140
apartments 132

B

Baðia Fiesolana (Fiesole)
.... 126
Baðia Fiorentina 45
banks............................ 141
Baptistery 30
Bargello 11, 19, 46
bars, cafés & snacks 7, 12
  All'Antico Trippaio.................51
  All'Antico Vinaio.................51
  Art Bar.......................23, 68
  Caffè Cibrèo................21, 96
  Caffè degli Artigiani 114
  Caffè Gilli.....................35
  Caffè Ricchi...................114
  Cantinetta dei Verrazzano......51
  Casa del Vino 12, 86
  Ditta Artigianale 96
  Dolce Vita 19, 114
  Fuori Porta 22, 114
  Gilli............................35
  Hemingway 114
  I Fratellini.....................52
  Il Cernacchino 52
  Il Rifrullo 18, 115
  Il Santino.....................115
  Il Trippaio di San Frediano...115
  'Ino............................52
  IO – Osteria Personale
    .... 7, 19, 118
  L'Antico Noè...................96
  La Cité.......................115
  La Ménagère....................86
  La Prosciutteria 52
  Le Volpi e L'Uva 22, 115
  Moyo...........................96
  Pitti Gola e Cantina...........115
  Procacci........................68
  Rex Caffè......................96
  Rivoire.........................52
  Robiglio.......................86
  Slowly.....................18, 68
  Volume........................116
  Zanobini.......................87
  Zoe 18, 116
Biblioteca Medicea-
  Laurenziana.....................74
Bóboli Garden 106
Bologna airport 140

Brancacci Chapel........12, 18, 109
Brunelleschi 29
buses............................ 141

C

cafés *see* bars, cafés &
  snacks
Calcio Storico 145
Campanile....................... 28
campsites 137
  Camping Panoramico 137
Cappella Brancacci... 12, 18, 109
Cappella Rucellai 61
Cappelle Medicee............... 74
Casa Buonarroti 90
Casa di Dante.................... 49
Casa Martelli 75
Cascine (park) 20, 120
Cascine market................ 123
Cenacolo di Fuligno............ 77
Cenacolo di Sant'Apollonia
  78
Chiostro dello Scalzo 82
chronology, Florence 146
churches
  Baðia Fiesolana (Fiesole) 127
  Baðia Fiorentina 45
  Baptistery......................30
  Duomo 11, 19, 22, 29
  Duomo (Fiesole) 124
  Ognissanti.................20, 66
  Orsanmichele...................50
  San Domenico (Fiesole).......126
  San Francesco (Fiesole).......126
  San Jacopo (Fiesole).........125
  San Lorenzo 14, 19, 70
  San Marco 11, 81
  San Martino del Vescovo.......49
  San Miniato al Monte ....
    17, 20, 112
  Sant'Alessandro (Fiesole) 126
  Sant'Ambrogio 18, 21, 90
  Santa Croce .. 14, 18, 21, 88
  Santa Felìcita.............20, 101
  Santa Margherita de' Cerchi
   49
  Santa Maria del Carmine... 109
  Santa Maria del Fiore..........26
  Santa Maria Maddalena
    dei Pazzi 92
  Santa Maria Novella 13, 19, 62
  Santa Trinita....... 15, 20, 58
  Santi Apostoli 20, 55
  Santissima Annunziata 84
  Santo Spirito 20, 108

cinemas 69
climate...........................6
clubs & music venues 7
  Blob Club.......................53
  Jazz Club......................99
  Space Club.....................69
  Tenax.........................123
  Yab............................69
consulates 141
Corridoio Vasariano............. 44
cultural centre 99

D

Dante Alighieri................. 48, 49
David, Michaelangelo's 78
doctors 142
drinking..........................7
Duomo (Fiesole) 124
Duomo............. 11, 19, 26, 29

E

East of the centre............ 88–99
East of the centre **90–91**
eating out......................7
electricity...................... 142
emergency phone numbers
  142
English cemetery 92
Estate Fiesolana................ 145

F

factory outlets, fashion........ 123
Festa del Grillo 145
Festa delle Rificolone 145
festivals 145
Fiesole...............22, 124–127
Fiesole.............................. **124**
Fiorentina (football team)
  122
Firenze Card 143
floods, Florence................ 94
Florence airport............... 140
Fondazione Salvatore Romano....
  108
food and drink 7, 151–155
football 122
Forte di Belvedere 22, 106
Fortezza da Basso 77
frescoes ....
  58, 62, 71, 74, 75, 76, 80, 84,
  88, 109

G

Galleria d'Arte Moderna 104
Galleria del Costume........... 104
Galleria Palatina............... 102
galleries................................. 23
gelaterie
   Carabé.................................87
   Gelateria dei Neri 95
   Perchè No!...........................51
   Vestri...................................95
   Vivoli..................................95
Giardino Bardini................... 110
Giardino dei Semplici........ 82
Giardino di Bóboli 106
Grande Museo del Duomo ticket
   27
Gucci Museo 38

H

health 141
history of Florence....... 146–148
holidays, national............... 145
hospital.................................. 142
hostels 136–137
   Academy Hostel.................136
   Archi Rossi........................136
   Santa Monaca...................136
   Villa Camerata 136
   WOW Florence Hostel........136
hotels & residenze .. 130–136
   Ad Astra............................135
   Alessandra........................132
   Annalena...........................136
   Antica Dimora Firenze
   ....131, 133
   Antica Dimora Johlea..........133
   Azzi.....................................133
   Bavaria.............................130
   Benivieni 130
   Bretagna...........................132
   Brunelleschi.............. 130, 131
   Casci 133
   Cestelli 131, 132
   Dalí 135
   Elite 132
   Gallery Hotel Art.................132
   Helvetia & Bristol 130, 131
   Hermitage 131
   Il Salotto di Firenze 131
   J & J 135
   J.K. Place 131
   Kursaal Ausonia.................134
   La Scaletta................. 131, 136
   Locanda dei Poeti 134
   Loggiato dei Serviti ...131, 134
   Maxim................................131
   Merlini 134
   Morandi alla Crocetta
   ....131, 134
   Mr. My Resort 134

Nizza.......................................133
Novecento 131
Orto de' Medici.....................135
Palazzo di Camugliano........133
Palazzo Guadagni 131, 136
Porta Rossa............................133
Relais Cavalcanti 131
Relais Grand Tour 135
Relais Santa Croce...............135
renting 132, 135
Residenza Castiglioni...........135
Residenza dei Pucci 131
Residenza d'Epoca in
   Piazza della Signoria......132
Residenza Johanna I 135
Savoy.....................................131
Tornabuoni Beacci................133
Torre di Bellosguardo...........136
Torre Guelfa 133

I

ice cream see gelaterie
information offices 144
internet access..................... 142
itineraries 18–23
Italian language 147–155

L

left luggage 142
Le Murate.............................. 99
Loggia dei Rucellai............... 60
Loggia della Signoria 37
lost property 142

M

Maggio Musicale
   Fiorentina 145
markets see shops & markets
Medici Chapels...................... 74
Mercato Centrale 5, 16, 77, 86
Mercato Nuovo...................... 54
Michelangelo ....
   13, 19, 31, 32, 42, 46, 74,
   75, 78, 79, 108
Museo Archeologico (Fiesole)
   125
Museo Archeologico 85
Museo Bandini (Fiesole) 125
Tesoro dei Granduchi, ... 104
Museo dell'Opera del
   Duomo 13, 19, 32
Museo dell'Opera di
   Santa Croce 89
Museo dell'Opificio delle Pietre
   Dure 23, 79
Museo delle Porcellane 105
Museo di San Marco 80
Museo di Santa Maria
   Novella............................ 64

Museo Galileo 20, 44
Museo Horne.................... 23, 93
Museo Marino Marini 23, 61
Museo Novecento 65
Museo Stefano Bardini ... 23, 110
Museo Stibbert 121
museum tickets................... 142
museums 142
Accademia 16, 78
   Bargello.................. 11, 19, 46
   Biblioteca Medicea-
     Laurenziana....................74
   Brancacci Chapel ....
     12, 18, 109
   Cappella Brancacci.............
     12, 18, 109
   Cappelle Medicee 74
   Casa Buonarroti 90
   Casa di Dante.....................49
   Cenacolo di Fuligno............77
   Cenacolo di Sant'Apollonia
    78
   Chiostro dello Scalzo 82
   Corridoio Vasariano............44
   Galleria d'Arte Moderna 104
   Galleria del Costume 104
   Galleria Palatina...............102
   Gucci Museo........................38
   Medici Chapels....................74
   Museo Archeologico (Fiesole)
    125
   Museo Archeologico 85
   Museo Bandini (Fiesole) 125
   Museo dell'Opera del
     Duomo 13, 19, 32
   Museo dell'Opera di
     Santa Croce.......................89
   Museo dell'Opificio delle Pietre
     Dure 23, 79
   Museo delle Porcellane......105
   Museo di San Marco..........80
   Museo di Santa Maria
     Novella............................64
   Museo Galileo 20, 44
   Museo Horne.................23, 93
   Museo Marino Marini......23, 61
   Museo Novecento 65
   Museo Stefano Bardini .. 23, 110
   Museo Stibbert 121
   Palazzo Davanzati 55
   Palazzo Medici-Riccardi ..12, 76
   Palazzo Pitti 17, 18,
     102–105
   Palazzo Vecchio 16, 40
   Specola, La................... 23, 107
   Spedale degli Innocenti 83
   Tesoro dei Granduchi,........104
   Uffizi 15, 18, 42
   Vasari Corridor 44
   Villa Bardini 22, 111

N

national holidays 145
nightlife 7
North of the centre.......... 70–87
North of the centre.......... 72–73

O

Ognissanti.......................... 20, 66
Oltrarno................... 20, 100–119
Oltrarno (central & west)
.... 102–103
Oltrarno (east) 104–105
Opera di Firenze
.... 123
Orsanmichele 50
Outskirts of the city 121

P

Palazzo Davanzati 55
Palazzo Medici-Riccardi
.... 12, 76
Palazzo Pitti.......17, 18, 102–105
Palazzo Rucellai 60
Palazzo Strozzi 60
Palazzo Vecchio 16, 40
Pazzi (conspiracy) 30
Perètola airport 140
pharmacies........................... 143
Piazza del Duomo and around....
.... 26–35

**Piazza del Duomo
and around 28–29**
Piazza della Repubblica....... 34
Piazza della Signoria and
around 36–39
**Piazza della Signoria and
around 38–39**
Piazza Santissima
Annunziata 82
Piazzale Michelangelo
.... 22, 111
Pisa airport 140
police 143
Ponte Santa Trìnita............... 59
Ponte Vecchio 18, 101
Porta San Miniato 111
Porta San Niccolò 111
post office............................ 144
public holidays.................... 145

R

restaurants 7
5 e Cinque 116
All'Antico Ristoro di Cambi.......
....116
Alla Vecchia Bettola 116
Antico Fattore 52
Arà è Sud.........................97

Borgo Antico......................117
Cibrèo 21, 97
Da Mario 21, 87
Enoteca Pinchiorri
....97
Fiaschetteria Nuvoli...........35
Gustapizza.......................117
Gustavino.........................53
Il Contadino.....................68
Il Guscio 117
Il Magazzino...................117
Il Pizzaiuolo....................97
Il Santo Bevitore 117
IO – Osteria Personale
.... 7, 19, 118
L'Antico Noè......................98
La Casalinga....................118
La Mangiatoia..................118
La Pentola dell'Oro...........98
La Reggia degli Etruschi
(Fiesole) 22, 127
La Vecchia Maniera...........118
Marione..............................69
Oliviero 18, 69
Ora d'Aria....................23, 53
Osteria Antica Mescita
San Niccolò 118
Osteria Caffè Italiano 98
Osteria de' Benci..........23, 98
Osteria dei Cento Poveri
....69
Osteria Santo Spirito 119
Quattro Leoni 119
Sabatino.............................119
Sergio Gozzi 87
Teatro del Sale..................99
Terrazza 45 (Fiesole).... 22, 127
Vini e Vecchi Sapori............53
Vivanda.............................119
Yellow bar 19, 53
Zà-Zà..................................87

S

St John's Day 145
San Domenico (Fiesole)
.... 126
San Francesco (Fiesole)
.... 126
San Jacopo (Fiesole).......... 125
San Lorenzo 14, 19, 70
San Marco Church 11, 81
San Martino del Vescovo 49
San Miniato al Monte ....
17, 20, 112
San Salvi............................122
Sant'Alessandro (Fiesole)...126
Sant'Ambrogio 18, 21, 90
Santa Croce ... 14, 18, 21, 88
Santa Felicita................ 20, 101
Santa Margherita de' Cerchi
.... 49

Santa Maria del Carmine
.... 109
Santa Maria del Fiore............ 26
Santa Maria Maddalena
dei Pazzi 92
Santa Maria Novella (church)
.... 13, 19, 62
Santa Maria Novella (museum)
.... 64
Santa Maria Novella (station)
.... 61, 140
Santa Reparata 27
Santa Trìnita 15, 20, 58
Santi Apostoli 20, 55
Santissima Annunziata 84
Santo Spirito 20, 108
Scoppio del Carro............... 145
shopping 7, 21
shops & markets....................7
Alinari...............................86
Aqua Flor...........................95
Barberino Designer Outlet
....123
Cascine market..................123
Cellerini...............................67
Coin...........................21, 51
Dolce e Gabbana (factory
outlet)..........................123
factory outlets..................123
Feltrinelli Red 35
Ferragamo...........................67
Giulio Giannini e Figlio
.... 21, 113
IBS.IT...................................35
Il Bisonte 67
Il Torchio.........................113
Luisa at Via Roma.............35
Madova.............................113
Mall (factory outlet)............123
Mannina...........................113
Mercato Centrale ... 5, 16, 77, 86
Mercato di Sant'Ambrogio 95
Münstermann.....................67
Farmacia di Santa
Maria Novella.............21, 67
Otisopse...............................67
Pineider...............................68
Rinascente...................21, 35
San Lorenzo market 21, 86
Scuola del Cuoio.........21, 95
Space (factory outlet) 123
Speziaria Palazzo Vecchio......51
Stefano Bemer.................113
Torrini.................................51
Via de' Tornabuoni........7, 21, 59
Specola, La 23, 107
Spedale degli Innocenti....... 83
Stadio Artemio Franchi 122
Stazione Santa Maria Novella 65
synagogue 92

T

taxis 141
Teatro della Pergola.............. 99
Teatro Goldoni 119
Teatro Romano (Fiesole)
.... 125
Teatro Verdi.......................... 99
telephones........................... 144
Tempietto dello Santo
    Sepolcro............................ 61
tickets, museum.................. 142

time zones 144
Torre della Castagna.............. 49
tourist offices 144
train station 61, 140
transport 140
Tramvia 141

U

Uffizi........................... 15, 18, 42

V

Vasari Corridor........................ 44
Via de' Tornabuoni....... 7, 21, 59
viewpoints 22
Villa Bardini 22, 111

W

websites................................ 144
West of the centre............. 54–69
West of the centre........ 56–57
wine bars 12
words and phrases (Italian)
.... 147–155

ESCAPE THE EVERYDAY

ADVENTURE BECKONS
YOU JUST NEED TO KNOW WHERE TO LOOK

roughguides.com

ROUGH GUIDES

Long bus journey?
Phone run out of juice?

👉 **TEST YOUR KNOWLEDGE** WITH OUR ROUGH GUIDES TRAVEL QUIZ

1 Denim, the pencil, the stethoscope and the hot-air balloon were all invented in which country?

  a. Italy   c. Germany
  b. France   d. Switzerland

2 What is the busiest airport in the world?

  a. London Heathrow   c. Chicago O'Hare
  b. Tokyo International   d. Hartsfield-Jackson
                              Atlanta International

3 Which of these countries does not have the equator running through it?

  a. Brazil   b. Tanzania
  c. Indonesia   d. Colombia

4 What is the principal religion of Japan?

  a. Confucianism   c. Jainism
  b. Buddhism   d. Shinto

5 Every July in Sonkajärvi, central Finland, contestants gather for the World Championships of which sport?

  a. Zorbing   c. Chess-boxing
  b. Wife-carrying   d. Extreme ironing

6 What colour are post boxes in Germany?

  a. Red   c. Blue
  b. Green   d. Yellow

7 For three days each April during Songkran festival in Thailand, people take to the streets to throw what at each other?

  a. Water   c. Tomatoes
  b. Oranges   d. Underwear